This book is ded

FORWARD

As we enter into the autumn of our life, it is not uncommon to "grope among the dry bones of our past." We look for the reasons we were dealt the hand of cards we received.

There are truly only two ways to approach our lives...as a gallant fighter or as a victim. Each one of us makes that decision, whether we are aware of it or not. In other words, will you play with own cards or play with a stacked deck that was dealt to you?

Curtis's book should be an inspiration to anyone who asks themselves, "why me, why now, for what reason am I saddled with this burden for life?"Curtis did not let the curse of FSHD, the abandonment of his father, sparse direction or guidance from his mother, or even the lack of a stable home environment detour him from finishing high school on his own. He served in the military, put himself through college earning a master's degree in the process. He even earned a pilot's license through his diligence of focus.

Read here, in Curtis's own words, the story of one who would bear unbelievable physical stress from FSHD, yet continue as a sensitive, erudite, caring, self reflective (warts and all) observant of world around him. Life takes a lot of courage, very often more than we think we have.

Curtis shows the reader the reality of the quote "Life isn't about waiting for the storm to pass, it's about learning to dance in the rain."

Curtis and his wife, Laura, live in New Jersey.

Steve L. Reist
(High School Classmate)
Kansas City Missouri Police Dept. (ret)

Author's Notes

As I was writing this it began bringing back long dormant memories; events that I hadn't thought about for a long, long time. As I dusted off these memories I began to realize how much I was enjoying this.

My goal in writing this story was to share my life's experiences as a victim of FSHD so that others who are faced with it will have some idea of what to expect. This is true of those afflicted as well as the caregivers who take care of them.

The day I learned I had muscular dystrophy it occurred to me as to how little I knew about the disease. Fifty years ago, I don't think many knew much about it. I had no idea what to expect. Frankly, I was getting along just fine and didn't dwell on it. The doctor advised me that it was a rare disease and I was lucky to have the type that was the least debilitating. I would likely live a normal life. Of course, that was the just what I needed to hear.

Facioscapulohumeral or FSHD is the most common form of muscular dystrophy. It is estimated that some one half million people are afflicted. Typically, it first affects the face, moves to the shoulder blades or scapula. It then begins to affect the upper arm muscles. Most often, it manifests itself in the early 20's. I had symptoms in my early teens. I would urge the reader to research the many details on the FSH Society's web site. I refer to this site and several others at the end. I am not an authority on this disease; merely a victim.

As in all efforts to create a book, I have many fine people to thank for achieving this. First and foremost, Laura. My beautiful wife of many years has had to deal with this disease nearly as much as I do. Perhaps she should be writing this.

I would never even have started this project if not for Steve Reist. A high school classmate and retired Kansas City police officer, he has used every form of coercion possible short of the night stick to get me started on this.

Wendy Serratelli also spent many hours of her personal time to correct this ignorant newbie writer. Thanks, Wendy.

Of course, there are many others deserving of my thanks. Thank you all.

There is evidence to suggest that we will soon beat this terrible disease. Consider joining the FSH Society and helping to eradicate FSHD. I intend to donate any proceeds from this book to the FSH Society. Life is good! Let's make it even better!

CHAPTER 1

I was born around 7 am at Los Angeles Hospital in California on February 7, 1942. As it was wartime, I imagine my father, Miles, was likely on duty. He was in the Marines. My mom, June, was a young woman of about twenty years of age. Supposedly, my parents met in a local dance hall that served to entertain servicemen. As with most of us, that period in our lives is only recalled by what others have told us.

Dad was not really much of the doting father type. Truth be known, I am sure that had I simply disappeared, he would have not troubled himself to find me. It later came to be known that there was discussion about putting me up for adoption. Apparently, Aunt Dorothy managed to prevent that. You well can imagine how that warmed my heart once I knew!

My father and I would never be very close. Most of my early memories of him were about discipline. I was corrected about almost everything. I guess it was his way of teaching me what he felt I should know and do. Many years later, I found out that my Dad missed his ship and was sent to the brig, as he was considered being AWOL. During the war, that was a serious offense. He was later discharged and as far as I know, never saw much of the war.

I am not sure just when we departed Los Angeles and went to Nebraska. Pictures indicate that I was still not walking my first time on the farm. As an integral part of my effort to make the reader understand how much the history of my family is important to me and what makes me who I am, I intend to take you back a few generations.

My great-grandfather, Sidney Baxter Higgins, was born in September of 1842; somewhere in New Hampshire. It was common practice in those days to send one or more of your children to work and learn a trade from a master artisan. Many families had more children than they could afford to take care of. Sidney was sent to live with another family at a young age. Likely, it was in farming but I really cannot be certain.

When he turned seventeen, he joined the Army as a Corporal and was assigned to be an assistant to a surgeon. This was likely somewhere between 1861 and 1862.

The New Hampshire Volunteers were brought south through New York and down into Virginia and fought numerous battles against the Confederates. Surgeon's assistants were expected to help in surgeries such as amputations and bullet removal. Often, there were no medicines, and no painkillers. Sidney would have to hold the patient down while the surgery took place and then clean the area afterwards. I would not have considered this a job with a promising future!

After the Civil War ran to its conclusion, Sidney returned to New Hampshire where he was discharged as a lieutenant. At some point, he made the decision to travel west sometime around 1865. He settled in Iowa with the intention of establishing a town and naming it Sidney. Since there was already a town named Sidney in Iowa, he decided to use his middle name, Baxter. Hence, the city of Baxter, Iowa was established.

Along with operating a general store, he was also the town's postmaster. The railroad was supposed to route tracks through the town but they were finally built a mile and a half south of the town. Eventually, Baxter relocated to its present location near the new railroad. That would be the start of the decline of the original site. The new site prospered and is still doing well today more than a hundred years later.

Sometime around 1880 or so, Sidney decided to move further west. He simply packed his wagon, hitched up a team of horses and with his housekeeper and young son, Edward, started out for Nebraska Territory. He left his wife, ?????, behind.

The territory was being opened up to development and was once again offering land grants to those who would improve on the land. This was done under the Homestead Act of 1862.

He was able to obtain two parcels of land (about three hundred twenty or so acres) in the upper region of the Nebraska panhandle. He was allowed to file for one parcel and his new wife (not sure if they were actually married) filed on the second parcel. His original intent was to establish a town, as he had it on good authority that the railroad planned to build through this part of Nebraska. It turned out that the railroad built the tracks 10 miles further south and the town of Rushville was started! His railroad predictions were once again, flawed.

He, with his woman and son, built a sod house and did sufficient improvements to be able to file for the title to the land. It was supposed to be a dwelling of twelve feet by fourteen feet. Trees were scarce so lumber was not available. Sod was the material at hand. The plains were vast and weather was harsh. The amount of land he had was not sufficient for productive farming so he found other alternatives.

Instead, he raised and broke horses for the Army on this land. Hay was also grown. The early years on the farm must have been difficult but somehow he and his family kept it going.

Years later, Edward took over the farm and acquired more land. He built two frame houses a couple of miles farther west from the original home site. He and his bride moved into the larger house and Sidney who was now alone, lived in the smaller dwelling.

Edward married a young schoolteacher from Pennsylvania named Ruth Bell. This was in 1903. They spent their honeymoon cutting and stacking hay! Ruth worked right alongside her new husband. They produced three daughters and my Dad, the youngest, over the next several years. Helen was the oldest and then came Dorothy. Audrey was the third born and finally in 1919, his first son was born. Miles Edward Higgins was doted on by his three older sisters, and being the only male child it is likely he was somewhat spoiled. Aunt Dorothy would later tell me that Dad could have gone to school anywhere in the world had he wanted to. It was not to be.

From this brief history, I could lay claim to sound pioneer stock. Determination to succeed and make a good life was apparent. I am not sure why that skipped a generation with my Dad.

Dad seemed to be born with a strong sense of wanderlust. He attended high school in Chadron, which is southwest of the farm and one of the larger cities in the area. He completed the prep school and soon met and married a young woman named Evelyn when he was only seventeen or eighteen years old. They were to bear two children; Kathleen and Gregory. This was around 1939 and 1940, respectively. Both children were also healthy, though Multiple Sclerosis eventually claimed my half-sister Kathleen's life. My half-brother, Greg, had no such health issues and is still doing well today as far as I know.

It is not clear just when Miles left that relationship but he next turned up in California. It must have been then that he enlisted in the Marines and soon met my mother.

After the Marines and after my birth, Dad would return to the farm and work for a while and then head for the West Coast again. This cycle was repeated several times as I grew older. I imagine my love of travel came from those genes he passed on to me!

I have vague recollections of when Dad was flying. Somehow he acquired an airplane, which he kept in a tee hanger that he had built on the edge of the field near the little house where we were living right there on the farm. The runway was simply a graded area in the field just east of the house. Later years revealed to me that he was a sales representative for the Luscombe Silvaire Eight that was the first all-metal aircraft of its type. This was likely in the mid-forties when he became involved. I do not know if he ever actually sold an airplane to anyone. My later research found aircraft of this type sold for about seventeen hundred dollars new at that time. That was a lot of money. I do know that my Aunt Dorothy got her pilot's license around that time, which was still unusual in those days. I was probably around four years old. It must have had a lasting impact on me as I dreamed of one day flying my own plane. I eventually would do this almost fifty years later.

I remember some more of the details when I was still that age. We were living in the smaller farmhouse that was originally built for Sidney, my great grandfather. It is a tiny frame house with two small bedrooms, a kitchen/living area and a coal cellar. Mom was due any day to give birth. It was February, 1946 and very cold. The windows all had ice built up on them and you could not see through them. When February 7 came, Aunt Dorothy had made me a peach upside down cake for my birthday. My next present I could have done without--a new baby brother was born! Bryan Brent was born on my birthday around 7:00 pm. We shared the same birthday from then on.

We must have stayed on the farm for some time. I recall the warm weather when I could play outside. I had a real passion for playing in the dirt. I would build roads and dams using small boards and cans as my bulldozers. I did not have many toys and longed for one of those steam shovels I saw in the Montgomery Wards' catalog.

There was much to do and see on the farm. We had a large garden with carrots, onions, beets, radishes and beans. I could pull out a carrot for a snack anytime. We also had rhubarb plants, which were somewhat sour, but I ate it anyway. Grandma used to can it for a dessert or for use in a rhubarb pie...good stuff!

Once again, we were on our way west. Dad had a Model A roadster, vintage around 1939 or so I would guess. He had built a wooden box with compartments that we used for a camp kitchen. It was hung on the rear of the car and had a table that folded down to hold a Coleman stove, etc. We slept in the car and camped our way across a number of states to California.

My memories of those travels are more impressions than anything else. I remember parking a short way off the road and setting up camp after a long day of driving. Coyotes could be heard in the distance and made me nervous. It would get cold at night and very hot during the day. The car would overheat and need the radiator topped off quite often. We eventually made it to a motor court in California. These courts were predecessors to the modern motel. If memory serves, it was called "Silver Court." There must have been some limited facilities as we stayed there for some time. I believe it was in Glendale, which was near where Mom's folks lived. I remember them a little. They were old! Grandpa Ellyson was an artist and painted with oils. I doubt that he was very accomplished but it is what I remember.

I have no idea what my father was into during that time. He worked as a car mechanic often and may have found work as a mechanic. This was likely around 1947 or so.

I have no recall concerning school though I may have attended one. I know I never was in a kindergarten program. I started in first grade. I remember when we returned to the farm, I had to repeat first grade again for some reason to do with my age at the time.

My health condition as a young lad of five or six was good. I was a scrawny kid but normal in all respects. There was no evidence of the muscle condition that would one day take over my life. It would be many years later before signs of the FSH Muscular Dystrophy condition began to manifest itself.

We returned to the farm once again. I do not know why but it was usually because Dad ran out of money or Grandpa Higgins appealed to him for help on the farm. This was probably around 1948 or so. I remember the winter was long and brutal as was typical of the Nebraska panhandle then and now. Blizzards were the norm. The farm still relied on the simple things of rural life: kerosene lamps, coal stoves, outhouses, etc. Our telephone was a large box that hung on the wall and was battery powered. To make a call, you would crank a handle on the side to get an operator to direct your call. It was a party line and anyone could and did listen in on conversations.

Fifty-pound flour sacks were made of a cotton fabric with assorted prints. The empty sacks were saved and dresses and shirts were made from them. True recycling!

There was no electricity until late in 1949. I well remember the excitement when the REA (Rushville Electric Association) sent crews to install poles down the road. I can almost still smell the creosote odor from the new poles.

Aunt Dorothy was a schoolteacher and drove to the high school in Rushville to teach.

On her way to town, she would drop me off at the beginning of the road that led to the rural schoolhouse. This was just a few miles from the farm. I was expected to walk to the one room school that was a half-mile or so down that road. I would walk to the school that taught the basics to eight different grade levels. There was likely only two or three in each grade. There was one teacher and lessons were often given by the older students to the younger ones.

Recess was always a lot of fun. Most everyone got along well. We played games such as kickball and dodge ball. After school I made my way home over the fields back to farm which was likely a couple of miles away. Sometimes the weather made me use the main road which was a lot longer. Sometimes I would get lucky and get a ride but not very often.

The winter of forty-nine was the winter from hell. It has always been described as the Blizzard of 1948-49. The panhandle area where the farm is, sustained more than twenty inches of snow in winds that ranged between fifty and seventy miles per hour. This happened on November 18, 1948 and lasted for three days. Severe storms followed on into 1949 causing even more misery.

Livestock were stranded, roads blocked, schools closed and everything came to a standstill. This happened over a four state area. It was around two weeks before plows could clear our roads. They had to wait for rotary plows as the drifts were often over twenty feet high! Bladed plows were nearly useless.

The military and other agencies flew aircraft with hay over these areas and saved countless herds of cattle and wildlife. There were subsequent storms that added to the conditions.

It was this time that grandpa took a turn for the worse. He had been ill for some time with diabetes and plain old age. It became necessary to get him to medical help which was ten miles south of us in the small town of Rushville.

Dad hooked up Grandpa's car to the tractor and put me behind the steering wheel with instructions to keep the car aligned behind the tractor. I had to sit on a couple of pillows just to see over the dash.

Grandpa was bundled in the back and Dad set off across the snow-covered fields looking for the easiest path between the drifts. We must have made a successful trip because I remember clearly riding in a wooden box smothered in blankets on the tractor as we made our way back to the farm. I was six years old.

Grandpa survived that ordeal but never regained his health and passed away a few years late in 1951. He was seventy-one. I found out many years later that he too, had FSHD. They knew very little about it back then and I was surprised to learn that the diagnosis appeared on his death certificate. Apparently, it did not affect him severely but who knows to what extent.

There were many experiences on the farm that became memories. I had free range to go wherever I wanted to. I remember swimming in the stock tank. I had a penchant for getting into the pigpen and chasing the pigs and thought that great fun. I had my tail section tanned when Dad found out about it! Of course, that did not stop me. Finally, one day when I sneaked into the pen to harass the critters I heard Mom calling me. In my haste to leave the forbidden area, I tripped over a rock and hurt my ankle. It turned out later to be broken and I had to spend the next several weeks in a cast.

The huge barn always intrigued me but I never really liked going in to it. I remember Dad had strung up a deer to butcher and it scared me when I accidentally came upon it hanging there. After that, I avoided going into the barn at all.

Many farmers in that region raised wheat as their main crop. Machinery such as a combine (threshing machine) was pretty expensive so it was common practice to hire combine crews that came up from the South. These crews would have three or four combine harvesters and travel from Texas to North Dakota cutting farmers wheat for them. They could harvest the wheat in just a few days and be on their way to the next place. I remember well the sumptuous dinners that were prepared for them by Grandma, Mom and Aunt Dorothy. This noontime meal was the main meal of the day and it was always big. Two or three meats, potatoes, vegetables, gravy, pies, cakes, and on and on.

The greatest enemy of the farmer is the weather. It turns on them in an instant. I remember well the times when the crops were nearly ready for harvest and a thunderstorm would come along and bring with it hail the size of baseballs! One can imagine what this did to a field of grain. Good years usually outweighed the bad years and that kept the farmer going, not always prosperous but independent.

Around this time following the winter of 1949, Dad decided to once again head west to seek fame and fortune or whatever other dream he may have had. It likely had more to do with getting away from the farm operation. It was no secret that he never really liked farming. Grandpa was no longer fit enough to run the farm so it was decided to hire a man to take over. His name was Bill Westerfelt and he lived in the little house we once lived in. He farmed the soil and was given a healthy percentage of the profits. This arrangement was to exist for quite some time. If my memory is correct, Dad never returned to the farm again other than some brief visits in later years.

We were living in a small house in Huntington Park, California by then. Dad was doing whatever but it was obvious that problems were nearing the surface. My parents would often fight. My brother and I would cringe in our bed while listening to the tirades at night. Soon Dad left for good. I never knew where. Mom was devastated. She found work operating a streetcar. By now it was likely 1952 or so and the end of my first decade.

CHAPTER 2

Huntington Park in the early 1950's was a well-kept suburb of Los Angeles. However, where we lived was not that great. It was set back from the main street behind an unused building and not very far from a huge steel mill. Our primary access was through the alley directly behind the house. It was cheap to rent and sufficient to our needs. We were lucky to have it.

My days were filled with playing with my friends, scouting and going to nearby Loma Vista elementary school. Generally speaking, I had few worries. Mom always managed to put food on the table, albeit a bit lean at times. Money was always very tight. If I wanted to go to the movies, it took quite a few pop bottles turned in at the local grocer to raise the twenty-five cents needed.

Once Dad left, Mom was the sole wage earner. Operating streetcars likely did not pay a great deal. They were still pretty common then but were slowly being replaced with buses. They operated on electric cables suspended overhead and rode on steel tracks like a train. For ten or fifteen cents, you could ride considerable distances. Too bad they were removed.

I had one good friend in the neighborhood that I hung out with. Freddy was my best friend. We joined the cub scouts together and rode our bicycles all over. My bike consisted of several different parts of bicycles that I found in the trash or was given by other friends. I would take the various parts and build a working bike that was not pretty or fancy but it worked. I became pretty good working with my hands. Over the years, my mechanical abilities would serve me well.

By now it was getting to be 1954 or 55. It was the longest I had ever lived in one place. Mom was still struggling to make ends meet and keep us going. It must have been hard for her. She still found time for me and my brother. She would wrestle with us and tickle us until we could not stand it. She would often read to us at night as we went to bed. I believe it was that joy of her reading to us that set the love I developed for reading for the rest of my life. I could not imagine life without the written word.

By now I am in sixth grade and starting to realize that girls are not so bad after all. I kept this revelation to myself for some time yet to come. My teacher arranged a field trip for the class. Mrs. Johanson was very devoted to her children. We were to go to Catalina Island off the coast of California about twenty miles or so off shore.

There was some cost involved but Mom managed to scrape up enough so that I could go. Most of us had never been on a boat of any kind before so this was an exciting time. I remember the trip pretty well. The island was very beautiful. We went there to visit an outdoor bird sanctuary where all kinds of birds were flying around. We were permitted to walk through the screened area and saw many different kinds of birds. I never forgot the experience.

My next two school years were spent in Carmelita junior high school. This was a big step in my life. My first shop classes were to further develop my penchant for working with my hands.

Besides all the normal subjects of math, English and geography, we were able to go to shop class. I cannot recall the teacher's name but remember him as being very patient and gentle with us. Our first projects were the usual small efforts to make napkin holders or small foot stools to take home with pride.

I clearly remember that before he would permit us to use a new tool for the first time, he would show short films that featured a character named "Primitive Pete." This funny character would show us all the wrong ways to use various tools such as chisels and hand planes. We all looked forward to these films. Many of the lessons still are with me today.

My first project in woodcarving was to chisel out the shape of a bowl using gouges and lots of sandpaper! It was sort of leaf-shaped and an inch or so deep. I suppose it was intended as a candy dish. We were cautioned repeatedly to avoid going too deep with our cuts as we neared the bottom. Most of us did just that and the teacher would help us repair the damage using a liquid compound that would harden. By the time we had the bowl sanded to his satisfaction and finished with hand-rubbed oil, the repairs were almost invisible. It was a good experience and we learned much from it.

Eighth grade brought more complexity to our projects. We had the same teacher again for the advanced class. Our project this time was to build a model sailboat with actual plans. He never hesitated to give us a challenge. Many years later, when I would teach woodworking to seventh and eighth graders, I would never have tried this difficult of a project.

The boat hull was several pine boards cut to shape on the band saw and glued together in layers. The overall length was at least two and one half feet long and about nine inches wide in the middle and tapered down to the bow and stern. The rough result was a hollow series of small to larger layers that formed the hull. Using chisels and planes, we had to remove the edges and blend the layers into the smooth hull.

After many hours, we had to make a hollow mast to hold the sails. This was about one inch at the bottom and tapered to about five eighth of an inch at the top. It was longer than the hull length. The ballast had to be poured into a carved mold shaped to form the keel.

We had to find enough lead tire wheel weights to fill the mold completely. We each had to carve our own keel mold in two halves to form the hollow cavity. This was a one-time deal as the molten lead (teacher handled this task) would destroy the wooden mold when poured.

Nearly finished by now, we drilled and tapped holes in the keel and fastened it to the bottom of the hull. Final shaping and much sanding would prepare the craft for final finish.

By now, you have a pretty good idea how much time we put into this project. The teacher willingly stayed after regular school hours so we could put in extra time. It was an exciting accomplishment and we were all very proud of ourselves.

That was when tragedy struck. One night the wood shop caught on fire and was heavily damaged. All six or seven nearly completed sailboats were completely destroyed. That hurt!

With only a few weeks of school left, there was no time to try another one. Instead, we were given the chance to buy a kit to build a completed archery bow. With the teacher's help as always, the kits arrived. The kit had two curved tempered aluminum lengths and several smaller pieces to make up the handle and provide attachment for the recurve portion of the bow. It even included a bowstring! Most of the difficult shaping had been done for us. We just had to file the edges, sand and polish the surfaces. It would be finished by the end of school.

We shaped the handles before the end pieces were carefully riveted together forming a bow about four feet long. The recurve shape was pleasing and it felt perfect in my hand. It had a pull of about thirty pounds. The handle area was wrapped in leather strips and we were ready to try out our first arrow!

That summer my best friend, Freddy, and I carried these bows all over to hunt for rabbits or whatever else came along. Of course, the critters were pretty safe as our marksmanship was pretty awful. It cost us a small fortune to replace lost arrows. Lots of pop bottles! I cannot imagine schools of today permitting such a project.

That summer also involved the Boy Scouts a lot. We worked at earning our merit badges, attended camps and we hiked and fished. Our biggest event was a twenty-five mile bicycle ride all the way to Palos Verdes and back in one day. To earn another merit badge was the goal.

It was a great time in my life. Boredom was never an issue. We still did not have a television set and staying inside the house was not happening. Neighborhood baseball, dirt clod fights, kickball and bicycling took up all our time.

I did not see much of Mom these days. She worked a lot and came home late bone tired. I went pretty much wherever I wanted to. I had to work hard at ditching my younger brother.   The more I tried, the more determined he was to be around; a universal sibling problem.

Girls were now a part of my life. My girlfriend at the time was a gal named Jo Ann. She was cute with her ponytail and poodle skirt. They would wear these frilly slips underneath so you could not get too close. The guys were all decked out in purple shirts, black pants and white buck shoes. Pink shirts were okay too. Our hair was usually cut short on the top and long on the sides with liberal use of pomade. We were cool!

We would meet at the local park building where the city recreation department would have teen hops Friday nights. I never mastered all those fast dances like the twist or the bop. I did like to do the slow dances though. I became pretty good with the two-step, ladder and formal waltz. The first time I danced cheek-to-cheek certainly released a lot of raging hormones. I liked that. Kissing was a bit of alright too.

There were many more first-time happenings during this time of my life that I will not record here, even if I could remember them all. In California at that time, you could go for your learners permit when you were fourteen years old. Mom had acquired an old forty-nine Studebaker car by then. I was not old enough yet but managed to learn some basics of driving though it was limited to the alley and to Mom's work schedule.

Jo Ann broke up with me to go steady with another boy. Of course, I was devastated and could not understand why anyone would want someone else. I figured I was quite a catch. Other girls came into my life and I recovered rather nicely. Sharon became the next in line. Then there was Pattie and Barbara and Janet.

There were other adventures and events that any twelve/thirteen-year old might have. Freddy and I were inseparable. We took turns staying at each other's house though I stayed at his house more often. He had his own room and was not bothered by any siblings. His mother kept a tighter rein on him too and preferred him home.

Scouting was still important to us. We kept earning merit badges and climbing in rank. I had hopes of making the coveted Eagles Scout rank. That did not happen but it was a goal. There were well over one hundred merit badges you could work towards. I had twenty or so and achieved the rank of First Class. Life rank was within reach.

We learned many skills that developed character and teamwork. I have always thought that the scouting program was and is an important part of growing up and learning that which we need to help get through life.

My final year at the junior high school saw me turn to ripe old age of fourteen. Various crazes came and went. I remember the yo-yo, hula-hoop, and braiding to name a few. I finally was able to get my learners permit and could legally drive with a licensed adult during daytime. Mom was pretty good about letting me drive as we went to various places.

She was doing pretty well for a short time and we would go to places like Knott's Berry Farm or to the pier on Long Beach. On one visit to Knott's Berry, we came home with a kitten. Tuffy was a gray striped tiger cat and he smelled from the candles at the shop where we got him from. He was a great cat and turned out to be pretty big. The good times did not last very long.

That summer Mom must have lost her job as we were once again in very lean times. She was behind in the rent and food became difficult to come by.. I always found something to eat because a large truck catering company was just down the alley from our house. There was a block fence about six feet high and a locked gate; but on the other side you could find discarded sandwiches and other foods. Apparently they could not sell day old stuff.

I got caught a couple of times but I do not think they tried real hard to catch me. I know Mom was really worried. It was a desperate time.

Mom must have appealed to my Aunt Dorothy. The next thing I know, it is being arranged for me to go to her in someplace called Oberlin, Kansas! There I would start my first year of high school in a little town of less than three thousand souls. Huntington Park was closer to fifty thousand people. I was fourteen years old. I did not even know where Kansas was, much less Oberlin. Bryan stayed behind with Mom.

Aunt Dot (as I called her) sent out money for the bus fair and off I went. Wow, talk about culture shock. When I finally arrived in Oberlin, Aunt Dot and Uncle Boyd met me at the bus stop and took me to their house. One hundred five South Cass Street...I will never forget it. This was home for the next three years. You could walk across the entire town in less than twenty minutes! All the stores were on a single street. The only tall structures in sight were the water tower and grain elevator on the edge of town.

There were not many kids living in town, as most were farm kids and only came to town to go to high school or weekend shopping and church. Adjustment was not going to be easy. I was out of place with California clothes and haircut. I tried to be friendly but was mostly ignored. School would soon start and I looked forward to the day about the same way you would look forward to a public flogging!

By now, I am getting taller and starting to fill out a bit. I probably only weighed around one hundred twenty pounds but had some sign of developing muscles. It was noted that I had rounded shoulders and winged shoulder blades much like my Dad. These were later learned to be typical of the disease that one day would be identified as Facioscapulohumeral muscular dystrophy (FSH). I was soon to enter a typical teen growth spurt which gave me more vertical growth but little weight gain. At my peak I think I managed about one hundred thirty pounds soaking wet.

Back to the first day of school, I had to report to homeroom, which was with a Mrs. Schoeni who taught freshman math. I had to stand up and introduce myself to the class, a group of about fifteen or twenty I think. The entire high school only had about two hundred students so classes were small. It was a credit to the friendliness of the Midwesterner that made this time in my life easier than I expected. There were some who did not take to me but most made an effort to befriend me. I remember particularly, Billy Machart and Roger Krizek being friendly towards me. Dale Miller was another that seemed friendly. We soon became pretty good friends. I imagine their curiosity about life in a big city and California was a conduit to this exchange.

School in the mid-fifties, particularly in rural Kansas was pretty straightforward. There was not a lot of room for the frivolous things like field trips and class parties. Another big change was that this was high school and the rules changed dramatically. Lessons were presented daily and homework was given nearly every day. We were expected to complete these assignments on time without fail. Coming from a western big city junior high school that was considerably more permissive, this was a serious adjustment for this California boy!

At first I balked and soon found myself behind in the assignments. I had never been an ardent student and it was becoming a real problem. Aunt Dot was the librarian and English teacher in the same school so I would catch it at home without fail. She would make me get up early in the morning for the extra time needed to catch up. Math was hard for me for some reason even though today I do quite well with it. It was mostly because I did not focus and tried to get by with as little as I could. My interests tended towards other things. Girls were not an immediate issue as it took some time to overcome my shyness.

There were some really pretty girls that caught my eye, though I would not dare call any attention to it. I well remember Robin Urban, Midge Huebert and Karen Anderson; all were real knockouts. There were others but suffice to say, I did not pursue. A young lady that I did eventually fall for was Joleen Miller. She lived in town within walking distance to my house. Of course, everything was within walking distance!

One of the things I learned quickly was that sports were big. Football was especially popular and the entire community followed the season closely. The Red Devils varsity football team was made up of at least a ton and a half of Kansas farm boys!

I noticed right away that most of the players had girlfriends and usually the prettiest ones. It seemed like a good idea at the time so I tried out for football and made the junior varsity team. As long as you could draw a breath and walk mostly upright, you could make the JV team. I soon found out that there is considerable sweat, effort and pain associated with this activity. I further found out that my talents did not lay in that direction. As my physical presence was somewhat diminished when my one hundred thirty pounds was put up against the one hundred eighty pounders, even my lousy math skills were enough to figure out the odds of my survival! Admittedly, my speed at running improved a lot.

Track was the next logical venture. At least in track, I did not embarrass myself as often. I managed to eventually win a letter and could wear the coveted letter sweater.

I also played on the JV (junior varsity) basketball team and did okay. I was tall and quick enough to manage not to hurt myself. Varsity remained elusive.

Truthfully, I only really excelled at spectator sports. It was a lot more fun to go to the football games and sit in the stands with a pretty girl and let the big guys beat their brains out on the field. The whole town would turn out for the football games. It was a much-loved event. Oberlin usually won more than they lost. Basketball games were also well attended. Many of us would attend away games as well. There was always a bus to take us to and from the games at nearby towns. After all, ways to entertain yourself were limited in rural Kansas.

By now, I had established a strong friendship with Roger. He lived on a farm just outside of town and had an old Chevy sedan that he drove back and forth to school. Saturday nights would lure him to town and we would meet. The "in" thing was to cruise Main Street and make fools of ourselves. We all did it-- up and down, up and down. It must have held some attraction though it escapes me now. Some stores stayed open later on Saturday night. By later, I mean 8 o'clock. This would sometimes bring out the girls in groups of two or three. Definitely a target-rich environment. As lowly freshmen, we were usually ignored. No self-respecting girl would even consider us sub-humans! Still, it was fun.

I became largely accepted into the Oberlin community. I did not realize it fully at the time but I was happy. Aunt Dot was always there for me and life was balanced.

Uncle Boyd was there for the first year or so after I arrived. He was a mild-mannered person that was nice to me but not a strong influence. He was a manager for a JC Penny Company store in another close-by town. It was the reason Aunt Dot had moved from the farm to Oberlin. It was a credit to them both that I never knew what the reasons were but they finally separated and divorced. Grandma Higgins lived with us in the Oberlin house and spent much time doing her crochet and needle point work. Now it was just the three of us.

A quick story before Uncle Boyd disappears was in order. Before he left for good, I had found an old Stevens single barrel shotgun in twenty gauge hidden away in their closet. Roger decided we should go pheasant hunting just outside of town. Pheasants were abundant in the area. They thrived on the corn and wheat fields and they were now in season.

I managed to sneak the shotgun out of the house without permission. Shotgun shells were easy to come by. So, hunting we would go.

I had no real prior experience with hunting other than terrifying a few rabbits with my bow and arrow back in California. Anyway, here we were walking the stubble fields with my single shot cannon that I had never fired before, at the ready. It was not too long before I made a bird nervous enough to suddenly and noisily launch right at my feet!

Startled though I was, I managed to get the gun to my shoulder and get a shot off. Naturally I missed. The bird had just managed to get airborne. Determined not to let my first pheasant get away, I swung the now empty shotgun over my head intent on clubbing the bird before he flew away. Missing the bird and hitting the ground was a given. The wooden stock did not fare well and I now had a heap of explaining to do.

We managed to repair the broken stock with some glue and tape and I slipped in to return it to its former hiding place. Home free? Not likely! I was nailed right away. Characteristically of Uncle Boyd, I was admonished about taking things that did not belong to me and told that had I asked, I would have been given the gun. Somehow, that was worse punishment than had I been spanked. Lesson learned.

There was very little change around the house with Uncle Boyd gone. He was never home that much anyway. Aunt Dot continued to care for both Grandma and me. She cooked great meals and desserts. She was still on my case about my studies. My grades were not very good. She expected and deserved a lot more from me but I simply slipped on by. Not failing but not excelling either.

My first winter in Kansas was a revelation. Snow, lots of snow came down. All winter. It was cold. I used to complain about the California winters that were rainy and chilly. That was balmy compared with Kansas winters!

I remembered the blizzards in Nebraska well enough but that was so much farther north of Oberlin. Well, when given lemons, make lemonade. I made pretty good money shovelling out driveways in the neighborhood. After doing ours, I was free to hire out. I made three to five dollars at a time and was able to shovel out three or four driveways a day. I was rich!

It was pretty easy for kids our age to make a few dollars in Oberlin. We had the advantage of living in town and there were not that many of us.

Shovelling snow and mowing grass was always in demand. I somehow landed a part time job at the Western Auto hardware store in my second year there. This was a great job that I would go to after school and work until four or five o'clock several days per week. I would stock shelves and wait on customers. I even learned how to use the tire machine to put on tires for customers.

The money I earned bought clothes and kept me in root beer and movies. Life was good. That second year I worked in the store throughout the summer vacation period. The town council had decided to build a museum to attract more tourists. Down on the end of Main Street they set it up. It was also decided to build a sod house on the property. There was plenty of room and it would exemplify life in Kansas in the eighteen hundreds. The people of the town pitched in and started this project. The stores were asked to contribute labor for the effort. My boss decided I should represent him and lend a hand which I did gladly.

Using sod plows that were over a hundred years old, the men would carve up the prairie and cut out slabs of sod that were used to build up the walls of this house. I helped lay in the sod slabs. It was a fine experience that I will always remember. I would not be surprised if it was still there showing how the early settlers lived. I thought of my great grandfather when he built the "soddy" on his land all those years ago.

Another way I was able to earn extra money was working on the farms close to Oberlin. One job entailed going into the cornfield after the harvester had been there. I would simply pick off ears of corn from the stalks still standing at the very ends of the field. The husks were dried out and very abrasive. A pair of leather gloves would quickly wear out. We were paid a couple of bucks an hour and were happy to get it.

Not all was work related. We played too. There were dances held in several of the kids' homes and we would all bring whatever records we had along to share. In the summer months there was a town swimming pool that we enjoyed. There was a local movie theatre at one end of main street that played what I assumed were current films. It was an ideal date with whatever girl you were with at the time. After the movies, we would go down to Wefsos drugstore and the soda fountain. The best draft root beer ever was served in copper mugs with sticks of cinnamon. Again, life was good.

Donna Jo Claussen was two years behind me. We hit it off and enjoyed each other's company a lot. Going to the dances, football and basketball games and the occasional movie kept us pretty busy. By now Roger had a girl too. I cannot recall who it was right now but the girls joined us when we cruised the main street on Saturday nights.

My schoolwork improved due to Aunt Dot's prodding. I was not likely going to be awarded any prizes for scholarly efforts but I was getting by. I enjoyed reading and that helped me. I also started to sketch with pencil and paper. I was able to sketch objects pretty well though mostly from looking at someone else's efforts. One of my classmates, Iris Graves was really good at sketching almost anything. I learned some from her that improved my efforts. Had I kept at it and gotten a little training I am sure that I would have greatly improved.

It was around this time when I (mostly Aunt Dorothy!) started seeing quite a bit of Dale Post. He lived on a small rented farm northeast of town. I do not really know how he and Aunt Dot became friends but I know he would help her out with things from time to time. He had three kids from a wife that he eventually left. She was apparently pretty worthless as a mother and spouse.

Dale would take me out to his farm occasionally to go hunting. I had developed some trouble with my right knee. I had excessive calcium build-up that made it pretty painful just to walk. The doctor thought it was due to the rapid growth spurts I experienced at that age. I was nearing the six-foot mark by now.

His treatment involved keeping the knee immobilized by putting a cast on my leg. Oh joy. This thing started at the hip and down to the ankle. I learned to walk with it and it did not slow me down too much. I even went hunting with it. Taking baths and laying or sitting down was always a challenge. Of course, it was not long before it started to itch. Thank heaven for coat hangers! After about six weeks of this thing, it was scheduled to be removed. It felt good to be free again but the smell was pretty gross. I eventually grew out of the condition anyway.

In the spring of the year I turned seventeen, Dad paid us a short visit. I had not seen him in years. He was living in Fresno, California at the time working as a welder in a vineyard. He had a black 1957 Chevy Bel-Air that I would have killed for then and now. He actually let me drive it out to the state park and back. That was so out of character for my father. Aunt Dot had finally let me get my driver's license so it was legal. I had taken driver training in school. In those days it was provided to all students once they turned sixteen. The school was loaned by the local car dealer a couple of new cars every year for the students to learn on.

Dad's car was beautiful. It was even a stick shift and pretty fast for its day. I had driven my aunt's 1956 Plymouth pretty often so I had confidence. It is one of the few good memories I have of my Dad.

There was the class play that I played a role in. "The House of Strangeness" was the title. It was performed for the entire school and the parents. I was getting ready to finish my junior year. Our class would be responsible for putting on the junior/senior prom. A theme was selected (Sayonara) and decorations were made to dress up the gymnasium. Iris Graves and I painted a lot of the scenes that were on display. Parents worked alongside the kids to pull this off. On the day of the occasion, we were dressed up and paraded through the town. We all wore flowers and looked our finest. The prom was a great time and a fond memory. When the end of the school year came my next adventure would arrive.

Dale Post left his wife and the farm. It was only rented and not very profitable. She had abandoned the three kids to Dale. He had to take care of his kids and needed a place to go. Aunt Dorothy arranged with him to take over the family farm up in Nebraska. He took the few tools and machines that he owned and made the trek to his new home. He moved into the little house where I had once lived and where my brother was born.

Dale was an early proponent of conservation farming. One of the things he had done on the Kansas farm was to build terraces on the slopes of the fields. The purpose was to retain water and prevent washout of the rich topsoil. The addition of fertilizers improved crop yields considerably. It was called contour farming as the terraces weaved all around the fields following the natural contours. Traditional tilling was simply going around the field perimeter or going up and down in straight lines. Contour farming was a bit more involved and difficult. It took getting used to and many of the older farmers resisted this change.

This technique was pretty new to Nebraska farmers too. Many of the farms were seeing their yields declining more each year. Soil erosion would take away the rich top soil and leave behind earth that could not support planting nearly as well. I remember well seeing the white knolls on the slopes of the fields where nothing much grew. Dale bought a used terracing plow and began to build terraces on the fields. The plow had a single large blade and an auger that was spun at high speed to throw the dirt up and away from the blade. After a number of times, the terrace would be built up and the erosion stopped. Some terracing by others was done with bulldozers and was faster but a lot more expensive.

Once they were in place, it would be several more years to build up the good soil and see yields improve. Fertilizers were used as well to help build the soil up. There was the main advantage that the terraces held the water when it rained. This held down erosion and served the crops. Later I saw aerial photos of the farm and the patterns of the terraces were quite beautiful. Little did I know that very soon I would learn more about contour farming first hand.

School would soon be out and I learned that Aunt Dot had made the decision to leave Oberlin and follow Dale back to the Nebraska farm. This was supported by Grandma I am sure. They both missed the farm that had been so much a part of their lives. I did not have much choice except to go with them.

I had grown to love Oberlin and really did not want to leave. I would be a senior next fall. I would miss my friends and the good times we had. Such is life. It was time to go.

The return to the farm in Nebraska was uneventful. A moving company did most of the work of moving the furnishings. We settled into the big farmhouse quickly. Grandma got her old room back and Aunt Dot took her old room back as well. I had a spot in the front room often called a parlor.

Dale soon put me to work doing things I had never done before. Most kids raised on the farm were driving tractors and other machinery from the time they were very young. I had never done those things up until then at the ripe old age of seventeen. Dale taught me how to drive the tractor and showed me how to work the soil. Summer fallow work involved turning the soil over to kill the weeds and getting the stubble from the previous season back into the ground. It was called fallow because it was not planted again until next year. By pulling, a machine called a disc behind the tractor the dirt was turned over. It had to be done again before a new crop was planted the following year. The main crop was wheat. Several hundred acres were tilled and planted on a rotational basis. There was winter wheat and there was spring wheat based on when the crop was planted. Winter wheat was planted in the months of September through December. It would start to grow but went dormant with the first freeze. This was necessary to happen in order for the wheat to germinate properly after the winter. It was usually ready to harvest by July.

Spring wheat was usually planted in April or May and harvested later on in the summer. Both types had somewhat different traits. The rotation of the fields had something to do with this planting cycle.

Harvest time was pretty exciting. There was a narrow window open for combining (harvesting) the wheat. Too soon and the grain was too moist, too late and the heads would lose grains plus the danger of heavy rains and hail that could come at any time.

Even the time of day could cause problems...too much moisture in the morning was bad. Sometimes, we had to wait almost until noon to start cutting.

My next experience was learning to operate the combine. This huge machine was self-propelled and had a wide cutting bar in front with paddle wheels that would draw the wheat into the sickle bar to be cut. That was called a header and was twelve feet wide.

There were bigger machines in use but this was still big. An auger would carry the cut wheat stalks to the center and up into the separators. There the wheat grains would be separated from the heads and sent up to a hopper behind the driver's seat. The stalks and chaff would be spewed out the back in neat little rows.

This straw was often later bailed and used for livestock bedding throughout the winter. When the hopper was full, a truck would come up alongside and the grain would be transferred over to be taken into town and dumped into the granary for transport to market. The combine never stopped and the truck would be moving right along side as the grain was transferred! This is an over simplification of the whole process but it was really something for this city boy!

I loved sitting up high on the operators' platform which was some five or six feet off the ground. Before that though, Dale took me around the field to show me what to do. There were hydraulic controls to lower or raise the header as the wheat height changed. You wanted to cut the heads off but not too much of the stalk. Typically it was about twelve to fifteen inches off the ground. You had to watch out for dips and raises to keep the sickle bar at the right height. Forward speed was just a few miles per hour. As long as you paid attention, things went pretty smoothly.

After several rounds with Dale, we switched places and he watched me for a few rounds. Once satisfied that I could handle it, he turned me loose and drove a truck for the rest of the time. He and Aunt Dot would take turns hauling loads of wheat into town. We often worked well into the night until it became too damp. It still amazes me the amount of responsibility I was given at the age of seventeen.

It was not often a farmer would own his own combine. They were very expensive to buy...even used. Dale was a very progressive farmer and always tried to have whatever machinery he needed. Some years the crops were just too much for one combine. Those years Dale would hire the migrating harvest crews to cut most of the crop. He would do what he could with the one machine. However, it was harder without extra help. Funny but I missed the excitement of harvest time. I still do.

After that, it was back to the summer fallow work. There were long hours sitting on the old Case tractor going around and around the field. It was boring. There was not much to see after the first million rounds. Occasionally you would see a badger or a coyote. The coyote would catch the field mice as I drove them out of their nests. He would follow the groove from the disc at a trot for long periods. For him it was lunchtime.

I started each day around five thirty in the morning and dragged myself to bed right after supper. Usually around nine or ten o'clock. A "couple of minutes" later it was five thirty again and another day in paradise began.

When I say boring I am being kind. The tractor pretty much followed the previous round with little input from the steering wheel. The speed never varied. To pass the time I would sing songs just as loud as I could. "Joann", "Donna", "Come Softly" and other songs popular at the time were vocalized in a most brutal fashion. Even the coyote forgot about his lunch and ran! My highlight of the day was going back to the house for lunch. I think it was this experience alone that convinced me that I would never become a farmer.

Another memorable experience was the round up. One of our neighbors just north of us had a pretty large herd of cattle that ranged over an area within the hills This was on the edge of the Black Hills and there were a lot of pine trees over an area of several hundred acres. It was not far from our farm.

We rode horses in and gathered up a couple of hundred head of cattle. We then drove them back to the neighbor's corral. This took the entire day to do and my backside protested mightily at the prolonged contact with the leather saddle. Still, it was better than the Case tractor.

Occasionally we would head for town to shop for food and other essentials. It was a real treat to have lunch at the local restaurant. Rushville was not very big and there was little to do there. I have vague recollections of living there for a short time as a small boy when Dad and Mom were still together and he worked as a mechanic.

The summer of 1959 was fast coming to an end. Sometime in August, Mom notified me that she had met a guy and was going to marry him. They had ended up in the California town of San Luis Obispo. This was well north of Los Angeles; closer to San Francisco. She wanted me to come and stay with them. His name was Jack and supposed to be a real nice guy. Aunt Dorothy and I talked at length about it. I could stay with her and finish high school in Rushville or head west. It was my choice. Aunt Dorothy sort of encouraged me to consider going to my Mom out of a sense of loyalty to Mom but I think she really hoped I would stay. Me? More summer fallow or the Pacific ocean? Go west young man! At seventeen my decision making process was no doubt flawed.

Mom had a friend that she was somehow in touch with and arranged with him to give me a ride west. Tony was somewhere back east and travelling back to California to look for work.

He arrived at the farm sometime in late summer. I remember him somewhat when he had briefly gone out with Mom a while back in Huntington Park. He seemed nice enough and agreed to let me do some of the driving. I liked to drive anyway so it was agreed to. He had an old pickup with a cap over the bed. When one of us drove, the other could crawl in the back and sleep. It was not half bad and the miles went by quickly. We made it and he dropped me off at Mom's new address.

I had not seen Mom in several years so it was a little bit strange for a homecoming. I met Jack and he seemed okay at first. Bryan and I got reacquainted and shared a room. Everything seemed to go along pretty well. I had to get registered at the local high school for my senior year. It was a pretty area and I thought it would all work out. Wrong!

The day I started school was an eye opener. These kids were something else. It was as though I had the plague. Maybe it was the missing silver spoon in my mouth that set them off. After the first week, even the summer fallow was starting to look good. To add to all of this stress was the transformation of Jack. It seemed overnight that he became demanding and obnoxious. I was berated for just about everything. He and Mom were constantly at each other's juggler.

Dale had given me several hundred dollars in wages from my time on the farm. I still had most of that. Mom helped me to arrange to buy a well-used Ford on time. I put the minimum down payment on this 1951 Ford hardtop convertible and drove it back to the house. Within a matter of a couple of days, I simply put my belongings in the trunk and headed south. No more Jack.

I was totally on my own for the first time in my life. No Jack, no snobbish kids, and no summer fallow! Life was good. My next question? Now what the hell was I going to do??? The old Ford was pretty worn and used almost as much oil as it did gas. What it did not burn it leaked out on the ground. It got to the point that I would buy cheap reclaimed oil just to keep it going.

I had made up my mind to return to Huntington Park and to what I had left behind back in 1957. If I had been of sound mind, I should have headed east and back to the farm. I guess the summer fallow issue got in the way of that decision.

A night or two sleeping in my car found me in the old neighborhood. I remembered where Freddy's house was and made that my first stop. It was almost like I had never left. I was invited to spend the night and have supper. It was during the meal when Fred's parents asked me where I would be living. What were my plans?

Have you heard the cliché of the proverbial pregnant pause? I had no idea. Quickly thinking, I mumbled something about enrolling in school and getting a job. I guess it was assumed that I was with Mom and they seemed satisfied with my answers.

The following day, I proceeded to job hunt. I lucked out with a Western Auto store nearby. My experience in the Oberlin store convinced this guy to hire me. Part of my problem was solved. I had a job.

Freddy's Mom let me spend a few more nights there after I explained that Mom was coming down from the north in just a few days. A little white lie but desperate times call for desperate measures. This gave me time to locate and rent a furnished room which I was able to do by telephone. I suspect the landlord did not look too closely at this arrangement. I paid in cash and he was happy. The room was not half bad and even had an outside entrance. I was not supposed to cook and had no refrigerator, so peanut butter and jelly sandwiches kept me going until I could afford to eat out once in a while. Meals scrounged from Freddy's parents were a very welcome change. They did not know about my situation. School was the next problem.

Somehow in my limited capacity for doing the right thing, I made the decision to finish high school The fall term had already started so I was already late. Not having any idea how I was going to pull this off, I just went to the school office and told them I was a new transfer student. I told them my Mom had to work so could not bring me. The secretary gave me a form to take home. "She" was to fill it out and sign it so I could return it the next day. I had to bring a copy of my birth certificate and my last year's report card which I fortunately had. Comparatively, getting job at Western Auto was easy. I was of age, had my social security card and driver's license , no questions asked.

Anyway, my very first forgery passed muster and I was again a student with a new class schedule. Huntington Park was huge, especially after attending Decatur County high school in Oberlin. There were somewhere around three thousand students in the four grades. In Kansas, a mere two hundred students give or take a few.

I had classes in math, gym, social studies, English and Spanish. This was my first class in a foreign language. The counselors had urged me to take it if I ever planned on going to college. In gym I signed up for weight training! I also had to have an elective such as shop or art. Shop classes were all filled this late in the term, as was art. About all that was left was choir or a musical instrument. I did not play any instrument but had sung in the choir back in Oberlin so the choice was pretty easy. That choice would later become most fortuitous.

I adjusted pretty well to the routine and became reacquainted with a number of friends and classmates that I knew before I had left for Kansas. I tried really hard to keep up with my grades by completing the assignment and participating in class discussions. It was starting to pay off with improved grades. It was not always easy juggling the homework, job and my social life. The old Ford was finally repossessed by the loan holder. I probably owed more on it than it was worth anyway. I was not using it very much as it cost too much and I lived within walking distance to both school and work. Several other of my friends had cars so things worked out pretty well.

I was pretty careful with my money and managed to cut back on the peanut butter and jelly sandwiches. We would frequent the local drive-ins for burgers, etc. after school or at night when I did not have to be at work. Additionally, the school had a pretty good lunch program that was inexpensive. They sold sweet cinnamon buns in the morning that were really good with a carton of milk.

Choir fast became my favorite place to be. The teacher was a young and energetic woman that really worked us hard. We became quite accomplished and were often invited to sing at local concerts, etc. She even acquired an invitation for us to sing in the opening ceremonies at the 1960 Winter Olympics! That was to be held in the Lake Tahoe Mountains well north of Los Angeles and we were to stay for two or three days.

Choir became even more a part of my new life. It was here that I met Jackie Rae Garth. It took me awhile to work up the courage to approach her...finally I did. She was a little slip of a gal about five feet two inches tall and would struggle to weigh a hundred pounds soaking wet. Do they still use the word "smitten?" If they do, I was. She had dark short hair and a pretty face. I adored her. It was not long before we became almost inseparable. She had a younger sister Mary and she took after her Mom in both appearance and mannerisms. I was accepted by her family. Her Mom was really great and treated me well. I do not remember much about her Dad. It was sometime later before Jackie became aware of my situation of being on my own but when she did, she became very supportive.

The Winter Olympic experience will always be a cherished highlight in my life. With a cadre of chaperones we were bussed up to the mountains where we were assigned several to a cabin. Separated by gender of course. We were watched pretty closely so there was not much opportunity for stealing a kiss. When we were permitted to roam around the Olympic village together holding hands it was enough.

The actual ceremony was really something. The entire choir was assembled near the unlit torch in readiness for the opening. It was snowing like crazy! You could not see more than a hundred feet. I do not remember that it was terribly cold.

As the Moment came to light the torch, the snow suddenly stopped and the sun actually came out. Doves were released and the torch was lit. We sang. All too soon, it ended and it was back to the grind. What a memory! Little did I know that, once again, my comfortable world was about to shift gears.

Soon after the adventure up north I somehow came down sick. I guess it was likely the flu. I just know that I was honestly and truly sick. I did not attend school. Truancy was not tolerated. The phone I had listed in my application was, of course, bogus. Not being able to talk to anyone, they sent a truant officer to check on me. I think this was sometime towards the end of January of 1960. The jig was up. When I returned to school I was immediately brought into the principals' office to account for this anomaly.

I explained to the principal my situation. I wish I could remember his name. He listened to my story quietly without comment. When I was finished, he sat back in his big chair and proceeded to explain what I already suspected was going to take place. First, I was without any adult supervision. I was a minor and so unable to decide things for myself. Law was clear that my situation was not to be allowed. His hands were tied. He then proceeded to inform me of my options which were limited. One, I could come up with a quick parent type that would assume responsibility for me. Two, I could simply quit and go find work. I guess he felt a certain respect and acknowledgement for what I had managed to accomplish so far.

He then made his final pitch. He cited my marked improvement in my grades and stated his admiration for my efforts to complete high school on my own. The final option offered was that he would promise to send me my graduation diploma if I entered a branch of the military service and completed boot camp. This was a new idea and I readily gave it consideration. I left his office with the promise to let him soon know of my decision. I wanted to look into this possibility.

Somewhat disheartened, I began thinking about the possibilities. There was some concern that I could not pass the physical because of the shape of my shoulders though my strength was pretty good. I was still muscular even as skinny as I was.

The Army did not appeal to me. They did too much walking. The Navy did not either; too much water. I considered the Marines but remembered the lesson from joining the football team back in Kansas. Not a good idea. The Coast Guard was about the same as the Navy. This left the Air Force. They were pretty fussy about their recruits but I thought I would try. After talking to the local recruiter for the Air Force, I was scheduled for a physical and aptitude testing.   No mention was made about my shoulders or scapula. When they found out that I was only seventeen years old, however, they told me to get my parents signed permission or come back when I was eighteen. The parent had to be present so forgery was not an option.

As my next birthday was only two or three weeks away and parental approval was not much of an option, I waited.

The day after February 7, I made the arrangements to have the physical and testing. All went well until the weigh-in. I was still only about one hundred and thirty five pounds. At six foot, I was about five pounds underweight to meet the minimums for my height. I was told to go home and gain five pounds and then return. The doctor suggested lots of bananas for rapid weight gain. I left to go buy bananas.

You can get pretty sick and tired of eating something over and over! My friends all had suggestions on what to eat to gain weight quickly. Many bananas, malts and burgers later, I again reported to the induction center. I passed the weight requirement by a margin of less than a pound and was given a final reporting date when I would be sworn in and transported to boot camp. I was given the date of March 30, 1960.

After informing the principal, I was free to spend the next several weeks working at the store and socializing with my friends. Jackie and I spent a lot of time together and grew even closer. I had found the need for a car so we could get around. I managed to acquire an old '50 Chevy Coupes. I think I paid around seventy-five dollars for it. It was not very pretty but I owned it. Mechanically, it was in pretty fair shape and more reliable than the old Ford. When I had to sell it I got most of my money back.

Funny, but I missed going to classes. Go figure! Thinking back on these times, it is amazing how so much could happen in less than year.

We were told to report to the induction center at seven in the morning on March 31, 1960 with a small bag of personal items and clothes. The night before, the goodbyes were very painful, especially with Jackie. Boot camp was eight weeks long and then on to whatever school I would be assigned to. After we were sworn in, we were taken down to the train station and put on a train bound for Texas. The Air Force sent all enlisted recruits to Lackland AFB just outside of San Antonio for basic training. We arrived in the morning after a couple of days on the train. I was homesick already.

The movies prepared me on what to expect in boot camp. Yeah, right. Suddenly we were reduced to sub-human status not fit for society! These drill instructors lit into us the minute we arrived and the bus stopped. We had not even gotten off the bus yet. After seriously questioning my heritage and ability to walk upright on two legs, I was directed to join in some kind of formation with the rest of the offal. We were then "marched" to our new home for the next number of weeks. After a quick stop at a supply building where we were issued bedding, we came to our barracks. They were ancient and the condition was as you might expect after thousands of recruits that had proceeded us had occupied them.

Clean but Spartan seemed to fit, and certainly well used. We were shown the correct way to make a bed and told to proceed as directed. After a short time, we were again gathered together in a semblance of a formation and marched to the chow hall.

We were given about fifteen minutes to grab something to eat. No sooner had I sat down to examine the mess on my tray to decide if it was edible when we were directed to take the trays to the disposal area and get back into formation.

I never did identify what was on my tray. I soon learned not to be too discerning. By now it was early evening when we returned to the barracks. The DI assigned one of us to the fire watch and the rest of us were told to get ready for lights out.

Fire watch was rotated among each of us and we were expected to memorize some kind of military code of conduct. There were ten or so of these rules and we had to be prepared to recite them if a superior came to the barracks.

Everyone was superior to us at that time. Lights were out at 10 p.m. and we gratefully hit the rack. It seemed to be about ten minutes later when the lights went on and we were directed to hit the deck and be outside in formation in five minutes! We were expected to make our beds, brush our teeth, shave, dress and be outside in formation. This ain't possible!

Our second day was filled with more fun and frivolity. We were marched more or less to the supply building again where we filed through and collected our new wardrobe, compliments of Uncle Sam. They gave us everything we needed right down to our skivvies. I had never worn boxer shorts before and after boot camp, never did again. Then with the huge pile of clothing in our arms, we were marched back to the barracks. We were then shown how to arrange our wall and footlockers. Everything had its place. Upon donning my fatigues for the first time it appeared I was going to have to gain a few pounds just to keep my pants up. The quartermaster must have been vision challenged...or just plain blind! Most of the others were fitted pretty much the same way. Our civvies were to be put into our personal bags and sent home. I really did not have any place to send mine and have no idea what happened to the stuff. I had other things to worry about.

Very soon, a routine began to emerge. Up at zero dark thirty; calisthenics, march to chow hall for breakfast and back to physical training. We would then march to the parade ground for close order drill. After that we gathered for a lecture on some aspect of military life followed by a march to the chow hall for lunch. Back for some more lectures or more calisthenics. More practice marching. All of this included frequent interaction with the drill instructors. They seemed somewhat difficult to please.

Afternoon classes were given on such subjects as military courtesy and conduct of the airman in various situations. We learned how to salute the Air Force way. Other topics such as how to report to your commanding officer properly were taught. Moreover, always the calisthenics! Displease the DI and you would get twenty or more pushups. I learned quickly to be as invisible as possible. It rarely worked.

I had noticed back in high school that my shoulders were somewhat different from those around me, especially in the locker room after gym or practice. My shoulder blades (scapula) seemed prominent. My shoulders appeared somewhat rounded and my chest somewhat sunken. My Dad was built this way so I assumed it was just a family trait. Little did I know that these symptoms were early harbingers of the disease. Even though I was strong and in good physical shape, when we were told by the DI to perform pull-ups, I had a hard time doing them. Stubborn determination made me stick to it but it was difficult. Chin-ups were a bit easier and push-ups were managed okay. I simply ignored this minor struggle and persevered. Sit-ups were no problem.

After a couple of weeks, we started to shape up and it got a little easier. We spent a lot of time preparing for personal and barracks inspections. Uniforms had to be perfect. Floors had to glow and the porcelain in the head had to glisten. We learned how to spit shine our shoes and the issued boots. These boots were rough leather when we first got them and by the time we finished with them, you could see your face on the toes! There were many more new challenges to come.

The shooting range was something most of us had looked forward to. Many of us had never touched a weapon up until then. Qualification involved getting a passing score shooting a thirty-caliber carbine at a distance of a thousand inches. Not much harder nor as much fun as the shooting galleries we had at the county fair back in Kansas. It was sort of a letdown.

Soon to come was the obstacle course and the tear gas house. The obstacle course was actually pretty challenging. There was even an area that they supposedly fired live ammo while you crawled under a barb wired maze. We had to swing over a muddy pond and go across the ladder like thing without falling in. The usual walls to scale and tires to run through were included. The tear gas house was another matter. I had no idea when there would be expectation to brave this gas in real life but it was a mandate here.

In small groups we were expected to put on our gas masks and walk inside as they filled the area with actual tear gas. Once inside, we were to remove the gas mask, count to 1000 out loud and then exit. The idea was that no one could count that high without breathing. They were spot on. I might have made two hundred before inhaling that gas and bolting outside for fresh air. Now I knew why it was called "tear" gas. Damn, that was fun!

After five weeks had gone by, we were getting pretty squared away. We began the second phase of training. I noticed that my uniforms were fitting better too. All the eating and exercise must have agreed with me as I had gained weight.. I wonder if that supply sergeant knew this.

With that we were given a bit more freedom. Sundays were mostly a day off. We were allowed to go to the Base Exchange to buy toothpaste or whatever. Our laundry had to be done. There was a cantina that served three point two beer as well as sodas and hamburgers and fries.

I had limited experience with alcohol of any kind so the beer was a new experience. On base we were allowed to drink the beer at the tender age of eighteen. We felt pretty grown up with this new rite of passage. We were also given passes a couple of times to go into San Antonio. This was a very pretty city with a rich history.

It was not much longer before we would finish up the training and be allowed some leave before going on to our advanced training. I had scored pretty high in the mechanical and electronics sections when I took the battery of aptitude tests.

I had several choices for training in these areas. I remember categories such as motor pool and electrician. A choice to train as an aircraft instrument repairman caught my eye. My love for airplanes sort of compelled me to make this my choice. The school was at Chanute AFB in Illinois about fifty miles south of Chicago.

It was the end of May 1960 when I finished basic training and was given ten days' time to report to Chanute. Most of us were also promoted to Airman Third Class and allowed to sew on our first stripe. The pay increase was welcome too. I recall it to be around seventy-nine dollars a month. I made more at Western Auto working part time!

With the next ten days of freedom, I was almost nervous to be on my own again. I was able to get a ride with some guys going west if I would help with the gas. I was on my way home and to Jackie. Life was once again, good.

I wrote and sent a copy of my orders to the high school principal that I had met his terms and completed boot camp. He was true to his word and I did indeed, receive my high school diploma.

I also found out that Mom had left Jack and was back living in LA. I think she had a job working in a small florist shop making flower arrangements. She was quite good at it. Eventually she managed the shop and was offered the chance to buy it.

It was good to be home again. I got to see many of my old friends and of course, Jackie. My mothers' brother, Clifford, lived in the Glendale area and helped take care of several horses owned by a friend. We were asked if we would like to ride them as they needed exercise. I had some experience with horses from the time on the farm.

I do not think Jackie had ever been this close to a horse before. She was game and was soon riding like an old hand. We had great fun riding on trails next to the river basin. Mom and Jackie took to each other and we shared in a lot of things in a short time. It was not long before my time was up and I had to report to the school in Chanute. Once again there were painful goodbyes as I boarded the bus and headed east. I would now have to complete instrument repair school. Several days later I arrived at Chanute AFB.

Each instrument type was covered thoroughly both in theory and use. Such things as altimeters, air speed indicators, pitot systems, attitude indicators and many others were made absolutely clear to us. We were tested after each block of lessons, which had to be passed with seventy-five percent or better scores.

There were forms and records we had to learn to fill out correctly. Everything had tags that had to be filled out and tied to each component. There were repair tags, back in service tags and disposal tags. There was a tag for everything!

We usually had the weekends off and could leave the base overnight as long as we signed back in by Sunday evening. Our barracks were much more modern than when at basic. These were two-story block buildings with rooms on two sides.

I shared a room with one other airman. The shower room and sinks were in a central area and shared by all on that particular floor. The inevitable inspections by the sergeants made sure the rooms were spotless and maintained to the satisfaction of the commander. All in all, it was not a bad life.

I made several good friends. My roommate, Russell, was from a farm in eastern Nebraska and we managed to catch three days off and hitchhiked to his farm. We were almost late in getting back but we had a great time. There were a couple of visits to Chicago but it was too expensive there.

I had saved enough from my meager pay checks and had purchased a small diamond engagement ring. It was modest to say the least but I could not wait to ask Jackie to marry me face-to-face. Probably afraid of rejection. Instead, I sent it to her along with my proposal. She accepted! I was ecstatic. She loved me! Now I was really anxious to get home.

Soon our training would end and we would receive our new orders taking us all over the world to different Air Force bases. Some would go down south to bases in Georgia and Alabama. Some were to be sent to Germany and some of us would be going to the Far East command. Our class standing helped give us limited choice of where we would like to go. That came after the direct needs of the Air Force came first. Germany slots were quickly filled. I had hoped to go back to the West coast but no slots were open. It was finally determined that I would be going to Itazuke AFB in Japan for two years. Oh wow...another adventure!

Being curious about just where my new home would be, it was time for a bit of research. It was just outside the city of Fukuoka on the southernmost island of Kyushu, Japan. It was the nearest island to Korea. Apparently, Fukuoka was the oldest city in Japan. Before I would see all this first hand, I had a full thirty days leave before I had to report to Travis AFB near San Francisco.

Once again, I was able to catch a ride to Los Angeles with three other airman graduates. Sharing the expenses was cheaper than a bus ticket and likely faster as we all switched off on the driving. We were all anxious to get home. We made it back in record time.

I remembered where Mom's apartment was and was dropped off there. The apartment was actually somewhat nice with two bedrooms and a small walled-in patio off the back. We talked late into the morning catching up on the happenings. I had not had a chance to call Jackie yet so was eagerly anticipating our reunion. After a few hours of sleep, I was up early and ready to go.

The following days and nights were filled with a whirlwind of activity. Again, my flawed thinking did not give thought to the long two years I would be out of the country. We were eighteen years old and in love.

I knew the short time I had left was not enough to arrange marriage before I left. I had no immediate commander to gain permission from and the AF frowned on young enlisted marriages, especially without permission. As we talked and planned our future, it was obvious that we had to wait.

Much too quickly, the dreaded day arrived when I had to leave. We talked and held each other long into the night and she drove me to the airport the next day. It was a bittersweet time. We both wiped tears from our eyes and said goodbye.

I left San Francisco out of Travis AFB on October 29, 1960, with a planeload of other military personnel. We were boarded onto a C-121 Constellation transport flown by the Navy.

The sight of seeing the Golden Gate bridge slide past the side of the aircraft will never be forgotten. I was homesick, lonely and scared of the future. I dozed fitfully to the drone of the four engines and read a little. They served us box lunches with cardboard tasting sandwiches and sodas.

Next stop would be Hickam Field in Hawaii. It was at least seven or eight hours before the islands were sited. They were quite beautiful from the air.

After we landed and taxied to the terminal, we boarded an AF bus and were dropped off at a transient barracks for the evening. We would be airborne very early the next morning. There was a mess hall nearby and most of us quickly ate and returned to our bunk as we were pretty tired for being in the air for so long.

The first things I noticed about Hawaii were the tropical beauty, soft warm breezes and the sweet smell of the flowers that were everywhere. Southern California has some tropical ambiance but did not hold a candle to this. I could get used to this.

Alas, after only a few hours respite, early the next morning after a quick breakfast, we were back on the same old, smelly, noisy C-121 and watching the last of the good 'ole USA slide away behind us. It would be two long years before we would see her again. We never even got off the base.

The next stop on this journey would be Wake Island. This was a coral atoll with about twelve miles of coastline. It was twenty three hundred miles west of Hawaii and used for a fuel stop. We had gained a day when we passed the International Date Line. About an hour east of Wake, one of the four engines just quit. That woke us up! Actually, there was little danger. It would take a little longer but they would fix it when we landed.

When we finally came on the island, the approach to the runway was all over water. Interesting sensation! Take off would be the same.

There was very little there to break up the view. The base was mostly the long runway, a couple of hangers and a small terminal/office building. While we waited for the refuelling and the engine repair we had to stay close by. After a few hours hanging around, a bus pulled up and we were told that we would be staying the night. The engine had to be replaced and they had to wait for one to be flown in. Wonderful!

After a short ride, we came to the transient quarters and were checked in. A small mess hall fed us and we were allowed to wander around the island. There were a couple of monuments to the Battle of Wake Island during WWII. We also saw a few old abandoned bunkers that were left over from that war.

It was late afternoon the next day before the aircraft was considered to be airworthy. With all four propellers turning, we managed to get aloft for the final stretch.

Several hours later, we were in the landing pattern at Itazuke AFB. We were in the air a total of thirty-one hours! Today, it is a fraction of that time!

Once again, we stood around looking at our new surroundings. The base seemed huge and was in a valley with peaks off in the distance. The usual blue bus showed up and we were hauled off to the barracks area that was mostly centered on the base. My assigned barracks was an old wooden structure of indeterminate age. We did not really have rooms but rather semi-enclosed areas that offered a bit of privacy but did nothing to curb noise. The latrine was again communal. I soon found out that they hired houseboys to keep the place clean. They even shined our shoes and made the beds. This was luxury! We had to all kick in some small amount of money each payday to help pay them. Well worth it.

We had a couple of days to get settled, explore the base and learn our way around before we had to report for duty. This place was a small city with everything one might need. We had a movie theater, a Base Exchange or BX where we could purchase most anything. There were small shops for laundry service, shoe repair, and even a hamburger joint. I can tell you the post office was a favorite. Mail from home was everything! It was a couple of weeks before I started to get mail from Jackie and Mom.

We even had our own enlisted men's club that served inexpensive beer and drinks. I think a cocktail was twenty-five cents. The NCOs' (non-commissioned officer) and officers had their own clubs as well. All the clubs had frequent shows for entertainment. Singers, comedians and other kinds of shows were featured. The Air Force tried hard to keep its men and women content.

We were in-processed, made to turn in our orders and personnel files, issued ID badges, paid and shown our barracks and where the chow hall was located.

On the third day I was to report to my new work place at 7 a.m. My assignment was the 8th Maintenance Squadron under the 8th Tactical Fighter Group. We supported two fighter squadrons of F-100 Super Sabers and one of F-102 Delta Darts. There were actually three squadrons of F-100's but one was rotated to Korea every month.

These were the primary aircraft I would be working on. Both were supersonic jets. Up until then, I had never been near this type aircraft before. I would be going on work orders with experienced techs until I learned all the systems well enough to perform my duties by myself.

After a few weeks, things settled down to routine. We rotated work shifts periodically. I did not really mind. When reporting for work, there would be work orders posted. These were varied and assigned according to complexity.

Some jobs were pretty involved such as fuel quantity problems. These were always giving us fits. Vibration, moisture, dirt and I suspect, moon phase would cause erroneous readings. Pilots sort of liked knowing how much fuel they really had. Of course, in systems as complicated as a jet fighter none of the instruments were immune to failure. It was rare not to have several jobs to do before your shift was over. I was gaining in experience and confidence. I was being sent on my own more often by now. I enjoyed the work.

We had plenty of free time as a rule. Unless special missions or other demands came up, we worked our shift and were able to do most anything we wanted the rest of the time. Weekends were part of the regular schedule but we still had our two days off.

It was time to explore this new and strange place. I would get with a friend or two and we would decide what to do for the day. Shopping, sightseeing and going out to eat were popular pastimes.

My first visit to the city of Fukuoka was something else. Little taxi cabs were all over the place and for a few yen, would take you anywhere. They waited in queue just outside the main gate and noisily competed for you to hire them.

Getting into one was just the beginning of the adventure. It was the opinion of most everyone that these drivers were all former Kamikazes' intent on terrorizing everything in sight but mostly us! Speed was flat out and the horn the main sound.

It was sounded repeatedly...not as a warning as much as an instruction to get out of the way...coming through! You could see the multitude of bicycles and scooters scattering in every direction. I wonder what their life expectancy was.

The city itself is a sprawling collection of little shops, large office buildings and Ginza's (cluster of larger department type stores) and little food stands. Of course, there were plenty of bars and nightclubs dispersed along the way.

There was a constant commotion from the hordes of vendors selling just about everything you could imagine and some things you could not imagine. I ended up buying a ceramic replica of a human skull from a little shop near the waterfront. This life-size replica was immediately given the name Hector and has been with me ever since. I still have him today more than fifty years later.

We all bought various unique gifts to send home. A popular item was the Geisha Dolls in a glassed in lacquer display case. I think everyone sent at least one home and of course, Jackie got hers.

We hailed a cab with the result that we heard brakes screech from at least a half a dozen taxis. We grabbed the first one and hung on for dear life as we were flown back to the base entrance. A typical day of shopping! Now, for that cold beer or four.

Other trips involved visiting the various Buddha and Shinto shrines that were nearby. These elaborate structures were set in beautiful well-tended gardens with Koi fishponds. The people were friendly and seemed happy. There was not much obvious poverty in sight.

Another activity a couple of the guys and I liked doing, was to go skin diving on some of the nearby tiny islands. We could borrow fins and snorkels from the service club. We would then make our way to the ferry and ride over to Shikoshima (shima means island) and spend the day swimming and diving. There were lots of fish and eels to see and the water was both warm and clear. Time was passing and new adventures awaited.

By now, I had a year in the Air Force. It was 1961 and I turned nineteen years old. I had to get an annual physical where the doctor picked up on my shoulders. Their shape was somewhat rounded and forward as I described before. When I raised my arms, the scapula winged out which he thought unusual. At the time I did not give it much thought. This doctor thought I might benefit by wearing a figure eight brace for a few weeks. This would hold my shoulders back. This I tried per his order but the results were of course, not going to work. I wore the brace for a while but soon discarded it. It called attention to me and interfered with my activities. I still had my strength and functioned normally as far as I knew.

It was around this time when I deployed on my first TDY. Our F-100 squadrons rotated over to Korea throughout the year for alert duty as it was often tense due to the cold war and the animosity between North and South Korea. Toss in the Chinese and Russians and you had a recipe for catastrophe.

We were assigned this temporary duty several times in my two years in the Far East. K-55 or Osan would be our temporary home. There were several diamond shaped revetments where our fighters were positioned fully fueled, armed and manned around the clock. The bomb load was top secret but rumors abound and unless you were totally oblivious it was a poorly kept secret.

Part of the rumors was that if these jets were scrambled and actually took off, they were on a one-way mission due to distance and limited fuel load. In addition, the weapons load could not be jettisoned and therefore, they could not land normally due to the clearance between the runway and the load. I suppose some of this might have been based in truth and some was pure fiction. I will never know for sure.

We were ferried in on a C-130 Hercules which was the transport workhorse for the Air Force. First impressions of South Korea pointed out the total lack of trees and the scarcity of buildings off base. It was cold to boot.

Once we settled in, we resumed our maintenance duties repairing the usual complaints. The flying schedule was much lighter here with only a handful of the Sabers being flown. Most were sitting on the alert shelters, primed and ready to go. Did I mention it was cold?

I had been in severe cold a number of times in my youth when on the farm and in Kansas so this came as a real surprise. There was very little snow but the air was humid and the winds blew constantly.

Airfields are wide-open spaces with little to block the wind. The temperatures were wide ranging between the teens and the thirties. That does not sound so bad but I am here to tell you it was miserably cold. Work orders that involved removing the access panels were a real joy.

There are a gazillion screws that resisted removal on each panel. Gloves were too bulky and not practical in small spaces. Hands quickly went numb. A routine pressure sensor exchange that normally would take twenty or thirty minutes would take nearly two hours. More time was spent running back and forth to the ready room to thaw out than was spent on the task.

There was another duty assigned to some of us. Alert guard duty on the perimeter of the aircraft revetments had to be rotated around many of us every day. It was kind of funny even if very uncomfortable from the cold and boredom.

The ROK (Republic of Korea) soldiers handled most of the main base security but only Americans were allowed near the armed aircraft. The funny part was when they issued us a side arm, it was an old Colt 45 pistol in a leather holster and web belt. We were given one clip with one round and instructed not to put it into the pistol unless really needed! I guess they did not want any trigger-happy guards with loaded weapons wandering around bored to tears. Keep in mind, most of us had never been trained for this and never had fired a forty-five before. Who knows if the decrepit thing even fired?

These deployments lasted for thirty days at a time. You could extend if you really wanted to. We were paid a small extra stipend for this as it was considered hazardous duty.

I chose not to stay. Mail was slow to get to us and it was pretty boring. The area outside the main gate quickly lost its attraction. There was a lot of poverty with children running around in the cold, barefoot and not much clothing, begging for change. We quickly learned not to give them any. It would turn into a small riot with kids coming from everywhere to surround you like hoards of ants. They lived in small shacks made of crates and tin cans taken from the base. Theft was commonplace. The only heat was from charcoal hibachi pots they had to cook on. It had to be a miserable existence, especially in the winter.

Back to Japan and my comfortable routine. I was to return to Korea several more times over the two years I was in the Far East but for now it was good to be "home". With the warmer weather my next deployment came up. In June of '61, I was promoted to Airman Second Class. Super, more pay!

The powers to be arranged for a good part of the Tactical Fighter Wing to deploy to Thailand. The pilots and planes flew down separately and we followed in our trusty Herky bird.

Prior to departure, we were all instructed to pack civilian clothes as uniforms were not permitted off base. We could only wear our fatigues when we were working on the flight line. They even gave us a clothing allowance to purchase civilian clothes. Good deal.

The purpose of the mission was essentially a training mission. The Thai Air Force would soon acquire the F-100 Super Saber and we were to show them how to fly and maintain the birds. I was to work with my counterpart and show him the systems and how to troubleshoot them.

We were housed in barracks that were built and used by the Japanese during WWII! These buildings were open to the outside and protected only by a short half wall and screening to the roofline.

There were wooden shutters for bad weather use. The tropical climate made the design quite practical. Even our showers were outside near concrete tubs that once were used for hot baths. Inside the open barracks the exposed wooden framework was home to various lizards that were supposed to help control the bugs. Best you shake your boots out in the morning to check for guests.

Once again, we had time to take in the sights and sample the fares of an exotic land. Dressed in our new civvies, we could jump on a bus for the several mile trip into Bangkok for just a few Baht (one Baht was about a nickel). There in the city, we had a choice of places to eat, shop and drink.

We were treated as royal guests. For most of the Thais, we were the first Americans they had ever seen and they were very friendly and curious. Surprisingly, most spoke pretty good English. I learned that it was required and taught to all Thais in elementary school.

There was also a heavy Chinese influence. Many of the small shops and stores were owned and operated by Chinese merchants. They loved to haggle over the price of whatever they sold. The initial asking prices were always well inflated.

A very popular product was jewelry with star sapphire gemstones. These were unique to Thailand. When held to the light, a four-sided star could be seen. They came in all sizes and grades much like diamonds do. I ended up with a ring for me and for Jackie. They were exquisite.

Food choice had to be done with some care. The Thais prefer hot spicy dishes that can be lethal to most western tongues. Once you became aware, there were plenty of other foods that were inexpensive and tasty. I managed to avoid the monkey kabobs. We sampled the various beers and drinks that were available. No real surprises there.

On other visits to the city, we would go see the many temples and shrines that were elaborate beyond belief. Apparently, Thai men serve a period of time in the priesthood. They become Buddhist priests for a year. Their head was shaved and they gave up all possessions They were easy to spot wearing the saffron colored robes. They had a small bowl and the people would give them food to eat. I think they slept in the various shrines but not I am not sure.

Another exotic feature were the many waterways throughout the area. These were called klongs and served as the main means of getting around and were like back streets.

A long dugout canoe like boat was everywhere on the water. With a strange outboard motor that had a ten or more foot long drive shaft; these things were used for everything from a water taxi to food barges. Saturdays, they would gather together in certain areas with an assortment of fresh vegetables, fish, poultry and many other things.

There were so many boats tied together, you could walk across most of the klong and never get wet. It was a common sight in the outer klongs to see someone standing next to his home on stilts, washing down his water buffalo as the kids frolicked in the shallow water.

Our workweek was not real intensive and we had a lot of freedom. As long as we were good guests, we were encouraged to make friends with the people. It was not a hard task. Very few of us got into any sort of trouble. Only one incident comes to mind that happened while we were working. An airman on one of the maintenance details had supposedly fallen in love with a Thai girl and requested permission to marry. It was denied as you would expect, so he went to the large hanger, crawled into a parked jet and pulled the jettison handle. It propelled him up against the roof of the hanger killing him instantly. Is life ever that desperate?

We were in Thailand for nearly six weeks before we returned to Japan. The twenty- three hundred mile trip was about seven hours of flying time in the C-130. Faster than the old C-121. It was a bit sad to leave Thailand and its friendly people but was good to go home again. Another adventure I will never forget.

Not long after my return from Bangkok, I had another major adjustment to make. This one was much harder. Jackie sent me the dreaded "Dear John" letter.

This caught me totally by surprise. This could not happen! We were meant for each other. Initially, I was filled with despair. The next emotion was one of rage. I was very angry. I threw away her picture and destroyed all the letters she had written. I wanted to erase her from my life. It was a long while after before I could deal with the whole thing. Time did its magic and I even eventually came to forgive her. Before that though, I did some pretty stupid things. Some of which I am not very proud of. I can place some of the blame on my tender age of nineteen, but only some.

Time brought me through this and I was able to move on. More times going to the city and nightclubs. A couple of incidences were burned into memory.

The gang and I were on the strip one evening going from one bar to another nightclub. One club in particularly, was recommended by some of the guys back at the base. Supposedly, the club had many beautiful women and they were very friendly towards GI's.

We entered and were seated and sure enough, several very attractive ladies made their way to our table. This evening held promise. Without going into the details, one of us found out that these "ladies" were actually MEN! Some joke. The second incident was to happen shortly thereafter.

Some of the guys wanted to hit the city on a Saturday night with the excuse that we had to celebrate my upcoming birthday. The leader of this motley crew took us around to several bars and we ordered the local beers and were having a fine time. This so-called leader then introduced the rest of us to a new drink he had learned about.

It was called Absinthe and was a very strong liquor distilled in wormwood. It apparently has a narcotic effect to add to its potency. I managed two before I was poured in a taxi and we caromed back to the main gate. I was told the next day that I spent the entire ride back hanging out the open back window emptying the contents of my stomach. As I said, some things I am not very proud of. My birthday was mostly a lost memory. I was twenty years old and life was still good.

CHAPTER 3

Days passed into weeks and on into months, and soon it was October 1962. I was a short timer. During our last six or so weeks before our tour was up, it was tradition to wear a Seagram's ribbon on your person. I have no idea where this originated but we all looked forward to displaying our own "short-time ribbon". Of course, you were supposed to have consumed the whisky in the bottle that the ribbon was taken from.

It was policy that men stationed overseas were to be given their choice of duty assignments when returning to the U.S. I would, at last, be back in Southern California. I selected Norton AFB and Edwards AFB as the alternate. I even started to think I might be able to rekindle the relationship with Jackie. We were at least friendly again by now. In about sixteen months I would be a free man again.

I had to out-process, including a physical before my orders would be issued. Again, some concern over my shoulders was expressed. I suspect I got through it all so they could simply pass the problem on to my next duty station. I had no problems functioning in my daily activities. My health was excellent with colds or flu a rarity. I very seldom had to go to sickbay. My strength was not noticeably different. I was not concerned in the least. Finally, my orders came down. I was going home...to McGuire AFB! Where the hell was that?

The Air Force in its infinite wisdom was sending me to New Jersey. This was about three thousand miles east of Norton AFB; so much for choice. Very disappointed, I managed to do whatever I had to do before I left. One surprise was the arrival of Dale Miller. He was a good friend from my Oberlin days and was in my same high school class. Talk about a small world.

We managed to bring each other up to date and then it was time for me to leave. I was happy to go. This adventure was over.

The return trip was pretty much the opposite of the first flight. Another gruelling thirty-one hours droning along in the old C-121 Constellation. Where were the new Boeing 707's they had now? These Connie dinosaurs were really showing their age. At least this time, the trip was uneventful. No engine failures or long delays. It was good seeing the Golden Gate again after so long. It was heart-warming...home again.

I returned to Los Angeles and stayed with Mom again. I had enough saved to put a decent size down payment on a 1960 Ford Falcon. It was a bright red compact with manual transmission. Not fancy but like new and got great mileage. Payments were small enough for me to manage.

Soon I met up with various friends, went out on dates and took it easy. Jackie and I were sort of together again but the intensity of our previous relationship never really returned.

I think the looming sixteen months left of my enlistment coupled with the distance made us both leery of commitment. I did not want to feel the pain of another breakup...ever.

Still, we had fun. We took a couple of trips and explored new places. The time passed quickly and I soon had to pack up the Falcon and say my goodbyes once again.

I had planned my trip to go east on Route 66 until I reached Texas and turned north to go up into Kansas. I wanted to go through Oberlin on my way to New Jersey.

I do not know what I expected when I finally arrived in Oberlin. It seemed different. It was smaller, somehow. The kids were in school and I did not see anyone I knew. I did not have much time anyway. I had to report in very soon. I had heard that you cannot go back. Now I knew what that meant.

My next stop took me to Offutt AFB in Omaha, Nebraska. It was a little out of my way but offered sanctuary. It was a SAC (Strategic Air Command) base and security was very tight. My travel orders and AF ID card gained me entrance and I was directed to the transient barracks.

The next morning after the first night's sleep in a couple of days, I went for breakfast, was able to get an advance on my pay, and was on my way again. Another twenty or so hours later I could see the New York City skyline in the distance.

McGuire AFB is about one and a half hours south of NYC and in a remote farming area some distance east of the capitol, Trenton, NJ. I finally made it and signed in and gave the duty sergeant my orders. I was now an official member of the 1611th Military Air Transport Command. MATs flew mostly Boeing C-135's, (707), C-130's and C-124 Globe Masters that would soon be phased out.

Once again, I had to learn about new aircraft. The planes I most often worked on were the C-135s. There was not much difference in the instruments, just more of them. The plane was a four-engine jet, basically, a Boeing 707. It was used for rapid transport of troops and supplies wherever needed-- a far cry from the C-121 Constellation it replaced. The Connie also had four engines; ancient radial reciprocal engines.

They were a joy to work on as the components were not crammed in tiny spaces like the fighters. They could be challenging to repair because of the miles of wiring but easier most of the time. Once again, after I became more proficient with the systems, I was selected to go on several TDY's. These short-term trips were varied in the mission. Some were simply crew efficiency flights. The guys in the cockpit had to keep current and we would go along to keep up the maintenance. My first flight of this nature was to Thule, Greenland. We were to fly there, spend the night and return the next day. It was a twenty five hundred mile trip one way. We made it in about five and a half hours. I had the chance to sit in the jump seat behind the pilots part of the way. Life was good.

Thule AFB was a very cold, snow-laden base. I understand the airmen only had to stay there a year at a time. That must still be a long time to live in those harsh conditions. It was still a great experience that I well remember.

Several months later, we were in an airlift exercise to Florida. Much nicer. Mac Dill AFB had fighters as I recall. It was near Tampa. These deployments did not usually last more than a few days or a week and it was nice to break away from the normal routine. I had never been to any of these places before and that was an added bonus.

Once again, our duties were pretty much nine to five or five to twelve. Weekends were usually free.

One extra duty was pulling KP (kitchen police). I had done kitchen duty only once before when at Lackland and I did not much care for it. We were to report to the mess hall around 4:30 in the morning. The permanent staff would assign us a variety of tasks. Peeling potatoes, taking out the garbage cans to empty and clean, or working the dishwashers. There was not much fun no matter what you did. I soon found a way to get out of this lousy duty.

I volunteered for funeral detail. Usually once a month or so, we would have to wear class A uniforms and travel by bus to funerals around the state. These funerals were for deceased Air Force personnel. I usually was part of the color detail that carried the flags. It was not real pleasant duty but seemed better than pulling the dreaded KP.

Dennis, my roommate, convinced me to go with him to the local college campus outside of Trenton. He had met and was dating a girl there. He assured me that it was a great place to meet girls. Turned out he was right.

I met Maryrose during one of these visits. She was a dark-haired Italian girl working towards getting her teaching degree. We were the same age and hit it off. We would meet at the Student Union and have coffee. Sometimes, there were a bunch and sometimes, just the two of us. It got to be a regular thing. I was working nights then so I could be there as I chose.

I, of course, just had to find a way to embarrass myself. It was easy. Everyone was supposed to bus their own tables and place cups and dishes in a near-by window. Several of the group had to go to another class including Maryrose. I volunteered to take the cups and saucers back to the window. There were probably fifteen or more. Two trips, right? Nope, let us just stack them all high on the tray and be done with it. There goes that flawed decision making again. You can guess what happened. They never made it to the window. A very loud crash alerted everyone in the Union, followed with much clapping and whistling. Great impression!

We came to spend more and more time together. She wanted me to come to her home and meet her parents. They lived in Hackensack, New Jersey in a large two-story house.

Hackensack is a suburb just north of New York City on the New Jersey side. When I arrived, arrangements were made to have me stay there in a spare bedroom. Her parents were really nice and tried to make me feel at home right away.

This was a new experience for me. A real home with parents that cared and doted on their children. Maryrose had an older brother who was a civil engineer and in Arabia. It was his room I was to stay in.

I soon learned that Italian parents had a strong bond with traditions and ways of doing things. They would have certain meals on certain days and it did not vary much. Mama Musto was the matriarch and pretty much ruled the roost. She was firm but very loving.

My acceptance was quick and without reserve. I was almost treated like another son. This was heady stuff for a kid that grew up on his own most of the time. I felt wanted for the first time since I had lived with Aunt Dorothy.

Maryrose would finish up and graduate before I would complete my enlistment. We spent a lot of time together and our relationship evolved into a serious commitment. Here I was twenty years old, and in a new land and a new relationship. Life was, once again, good. Time passed and she was finished with college. I still had some long months to go before my discharge.

My work schedule allowed my weekends to be free most of the time. I had a standing invitation to come to Hackensack and stay the weekends. It was a two plus hour ride up the Turnpike but I looked forward to it. We went out and I made new friends. I met her cousins, aunts and uncles. There were a lot of them. Birthdays were celebrated. They held parties for special occasions. Sometime during this period, I turned twenty-one years old. At least now I could buy a drink legally. We planned for our future which looked pretty good. For the first time that I could remember, I had direction and purpose. It was a pretty good feeling.

Four years to the day, March 31, 1964, I was honorably discharged from the Air Force. I still had two years of inactive reserve time to serve but it was not to affect my life. I missed being extended on my enlistment because of the looming Vietnam war by less than 3 months. I left McGuire for the final time and drove to my new home. Another adventure awaited.

I was able to find work quickly. A small company located in NY state not that far from Hackensack hired me on as an engineering technician. Materials Research Corporation prepared metallurgical samples for universities and other research organizations. Rare earth metals were processed in various ways and sent out.

One of my first jobs was to learn how to run what they called a zone refiner. Simply put, this was a high voltage. high vacuum system that allowed a rod of metal such as titanium to be processed into a single pure crystal form.

The vacuum chamber used a hot oil process to develop vacuums greater even than outer space. By literally melting a "zone" on a rod of metal using a tungsten filament driven by very high current, I would then raise this molten zone up the length of the rod very slowly. When finished, the result was a realignment of the molecules leaving a perfect large single crystal the length of the rod. This was a very desirable phenomenon that did not occur naturally. It had many potential industrial applications that were beyond my limited understanding.

I became quite proficient at this process. My boss was the project engineer and became a sort of mentor. He taught me much about the science of metallurgy and challenged me often with his projects.

He was adamant that I should to go to a school of higher learning and stated that upon completion, I could always come back and he would have a position waiting.

Until that discussion, I do not think I had ever given much thought to going to college. I just was not that smart. I did not pursue this beyond that point for more than another year or so. This would change.

In the meantime, as I had turned twenty-one years old I was to receive a fifty-dollar check in the mail from Aunt Dorothy. During my wild teens, she had bet me that I would be married before I could turn twenty-one. I was way too girl crazy! Somehow I won but not by much.

In the meantime, November 1964 rolled around and it was time for the wedding. Maryrose had been teaching in her second year by now. She taught classes in a Hackensack elementary school. We had planned on our wedding mostly by ourselves. Her folks had provided her with an education that left very little to fund a fancy wedding. I would have been okay going to the courthouse but she was adamant that she wanted the big wedding thing. We would pay for our own and it would be perfect.

I had no one of my family around so the guest list consisted mostly of her family. My Mom said she would try to make it but of course, it did not happen. While I was in on the discussions about the guest list, I mostly just listened as the two of them argued about who should be invited. Before it was finalized, the list had grown to some one hundred twenty five guests. We were able to find a really nice place nearby to have our reception. These places were in demand and arrangements had to be made months in advance. We were fortunate only because a November wedding is not as popular.

There were a number of considerations that had to be dealt with before the nuptials. I was born and raised as a protestant Methodist. She was a strong Catholic girl. In the interest of expediency, I simply converted to Catholicism. I have never been one who would be considered deeply religious. I believe in Him but man and his beliefs often leave more questions than answers. I tried to do what was expected of me but it was always in the back of my mind that I just did not buy into what was being offered.

The church was only up the street from the house and after several visits with the priest for what they called Pre-Cana instruction we were ready for marriage. This from a priest that had never been married nor ever would be. Strange!

The big day finally arrived and I was dressed up in a tuxedo for the first time in my life. Maryrose had a real good friend who happened to live nearby. Her friend Mary and her husband, Alan, were the best couple.

Alan and I had become pretty good friends in a fairly short time. He liked hunting and got me started in hunting in this area. He was an easy choice to stand up for me.

The church ceremony was really nice and very traditional. Maryrose was radiant in her white gown.

Me, I suffered through the so-called morning suit or tuxedo. I initially thought that it was a mourning suit which sort of seemed a better name.

After a long drawn out mass and our vows were exchanged, we descended the church steps towards the limo as we were pelted with rice. We then entered an area next to the church to have a bunch of pictures taken of the bridal party while the rest of the guests made their way to the reception.

We finally arrived at the reception hall and entered a private room to await our grand entrance. With much fanfare and noise, we followed the wedding party in and went to our table. It was an evening of food and drink ending with a reception line. Here the guests lined up to offer their good wishes and usually a gift envelope. This brought the occasion to a close. I had learned that most wedding gifts were cash rather than actual items. Frankly, it was most welcome. This had been a very expensive day!

We took a short honeymoon trip to Niagara Falls and were soon again at our jobs. Her parents offered us the top floor of the two family house and they moved downstairs with grandma. Her grandpa had passed away before my time. We had plenty of room with two bedrooms, eat-in kitchen and a large living room. It was comfortable. Rooms were painted and new curtains hung and life moved on. My first Christmas there was an eye opener.

When I was growing up, Christmas was a time to go to church and have a nice dinner afterwards. Gifts were few and not really important anyway. We never had much extra money to squander on stuff we did not really need.

I can only remember two gifts that I received as a child that were special. Once when I was about seven, I was given a toy steam shovel. It was big and blue and yellow. I loved it. Again, around ten years old, I got my first bicycle. It was a well-used bike that Dad had repainted. It looked new to me and I rode it everywhere. Most gifts I received growing up were clothes that I needed. That is the way it was.

In Hackensack it was very different. Everyone had to get gifts for everyone else. The tree was easily seven feet tall and there had to be well over a hundred gifts under it by the time Christmas arrived. Even friends bought gifts and received them in return. I did not really know what to make of it all.

Life settled down to the usual routines as we went to work and enjoyed the time off together. My twenty-second birthday came and went and then my first son arrived. This was May 25, 1965 and we named him Craig Alan. Talk about life events. This was a definite!

I still did not make a lot of money. It was around eighty-five dollars a week, as I recall. Maryrose made a bit more but that was gone for a while until she went back after the birth.

We were fortunate that her folks were good to us. We paid rent on the apartment but it was reasonable. Other expenses were relatively low. Soon, she went back to her teaching job and things returned to more or less normal.

Her Mom took care of Craig until she got home. All in all, life was pretty good. The problems were manageable and things continued to get better.

I was still enjoying my job and being given more complex tasks. I worked in the research and development area and was assigned all kinds of different jobs to do. Some days I would be on the zone refiners and other days assembling electronic circuits or tearing down a vacuum pump system. I also spent time in the back manufacturing area. Here they fabricated everything needed for use on vacuum systems. Large aluminum or stainless steel rings were machined with ports bored so that different tools could be used while under ultra-high vacuums. These were sold to other research organizations. We also manufactured and assembled complete zone refiners that were sold to various research universities. For a small company, we were pretty busy.

There was no tech support department per se. One assignment I remember was being asked to install and set up a zone refiner out on Long Island, almost at the very end. Brookhaven National Laboratories was a nuclear power research facility. The building where I would install the machine was cavernous. They had an actual reactor within and it was operational. Everything was huge and precautions were emphasized to the point that it made me somewhat nervous. I came back unscathed and did not glow in the dark so all was well. It was an interesting day.

Maryrose and I managed to arrange to buy our first new car around this time. It was a factory ordered 1966 Chevy Hardtop. It was maroon and sported a huge 396 cubic inch engine turning out well over three hundred horsepower. I loved it! It was fast, sporty and a blast to drive. Of course gas was pretty high at around thirty-two cents per gallon.

At some point I ended up with an appointment with Dr. Lebowitz. He was a GP that my wife had been going to. There was a growing concern about my shoulders and arms. I had noticed some signs that things were not as they should be. It took a little more effort to lift things over my head. I thought the muscles of my upper right arm were a bit smaller; especially my triceps. The doctor was reassuring but wanted to look into it closer. No determination was made right away. Sometime later, I was scheduled into Hackensack Hospital for a muscle biopsy from my left shoulder. I was also examined by a neurologist. The biopsy was no big deal. I watched as they numbed the area and cut a small opening to remove a piece of muscle tissue for close examination. A few stitches and dressing and I was on my way home.

A few days later, the good doctor called us into his office. His preliminary findings pointed to a condition called FSH muscular dystrophy.

He stated he was not absolutely sure and would continue to work on it.

He went on to explain that FSHD (Facioscapulohumeral Muscular Dystrophy) was a fairly rare disease of the muscles in the upper arm, face and shoulder blades. It was supposed to be a very slow progression of muscle loss that would most likely permit me a normal life.

Scared but with a renewed hope, I began to reconsider the idea of college. It was in early 1967 when the diagnosis was pretty well confirmed. It was at this time that I found out from Aunt Dorothy that Grandpa Edward Higgins had the same diagnosis. Later, it was determined that my father also had it. Obviously, the level of affliction was a variable. My brother Bryan showed no symptoms at all.

On May 13th of that year, my second son arrived. We named him Scott Christopher. My family was growing. When Craig was born, I remembered different feelings and emotions. I was proud, scared, worried, and very unsure of myself. Maryrose took to motherhood like a duck to water.

Fatherhood was not the same for me. Diapers were to be avoided at all costs. The wet ones I could deal with but if it turned out otherwise, I was in big trouble! I had to pretty much learn to do this holding my breath and mostly blind. A two-minute task could take twenty minutes. With the latest arrival, one would think I would be an old hand at this stuff. Nope, diapers had not gotten any easier by one iota. I could hold my breath a little longer though.

Maryrose was pretty darned efficient with giving birth. The first one had her in labor for less than two hours before Craig popped into the world. Scott very nearly did not wait to get to the hospital before he made his entrance. Of course, I was in absolute control at all times and had the situation well in hand! Sure I did.

Concerned about the cost of college, I found out that the GI Bill would pay part of my expenses for school. That would help. I had hoped I might enter into an engineering program but there were only a few colleges that offered that and they were more expensive and farther away. In addition, my grade history while in high school was not up to par with the prerequisites for engineering studies. I did not have enough advanced math or the two-year foreign language requirement.

I had gone to visit Montclair State Teachers College not too far away. After viewing my records, they told me of my deficiencies. Because I was a military veteran, they agreed to let me take the entrance exam. If I passed this, I could apply to the Industrial Arts program and earn my degree and teaching certificate to become a shop teacher. I did indeed do well with the testing and true to their word; I was accepted as a provisional student in the Industrial Arts department. I had a few months before the fall semester began and arrangements had to be made. I knew I would have to do well with my grades that first year before I could lose the provisional status.

I would soon leave MRC after I had advised my boss of my intentions to start school in the fall. I would be missed but he agreed it was the best course of action for me. He told me I would always have a job there if I wanted it. I really hated to leave. After my two-week notice, I was a free agent again.

I did finish my two-year reserve obligation to the Air Force and received my final notice of service termination. I had not given it any thought anyway.

I would still need to work even if only part time. With a growing family bills were still piling up and we needed food on the table. I had filled out a job application with the U.S. Post Office and had high hopes that would come through. It paid pretty well and hours were flexible. It was certainly a worrisome time. I was determined to go to school but would not neglect my family obligations to do so. Truthfully, I was pretty strung out.

Maryrose's uncle came through and offered me a job driving a truck for his company for the summer. He was the shop steward with the Teamsters Union. I would be able to work as a fill-in driver without having to join the union. It was a short-term position but would help. I was to drive the truck routes for guys that went on vacation or were absent for whatever the reason.

My time driving a truck on the farm hauling wheat would come in handy. I worked nearly every day going on different routes delivering many different things. Driving a big truck in this area was far different than driving one on the farm.

Heavy traffic and congested roads were the norm. Deliveries were often in difficult places to get to and on narrow streets with no parking to be had. It was a joy if I got a delivery to a warehouse that had loading docks and forklifts. Still, it paid well and often. I got paid cash at the end of every day I worked.

Towards the end of summer, with school nearing, I was notified that I could begin as a temporary mail clerk in the Postal Sectional Center. I would be working in the South Hackensack facility only a few blocks away from where we lived. Temporary status meant that I could work flexible hours and not interfere with my school schedule. Typically, I would start around four in the afternoon and work until eleven thirty at night. Things were working out pretty well.

Prior to classes starting, we had to attend orientation which was supposed to prepare us for the life of academia. We also had to register for the various classes that were required and elective. Freshmen had to take certain courses such as English, Mathematics, History, and Science.. A full class load was considered to be between twelve and fifteen credit points per semester. Most of the required classes were two or three credits and electives varied as well. I kept my first year at around twelve credits to give myself a chance to get back into the traces. It had been a long time since high school and my study habits had to be redeveloped.

There would be very little pressure from the instructors here. You were on your own. If you were not prepared, it was simply marked on their records. At some point if you were in danger of failing, they would send a notice home but it was entirely dependent on you to seek help or discipline yourself as needed. In other words, it was totally up to the student as to the level of success he or she would have in their college career.

If I completed the Freshman year with a GPA (grade point average) of two point five or better, I would be able to matriculate into the program and lose the probationary status. Always in the back of my mind was the fact that my success in high school was less than exemplary and the same would not be tolerated here. Most of my fellow students were four or five years younger than I and fresh from high school. They did not have a family to take care of. Well, no sense in whining.

As the saying goes, "nothing ventured, nothing gained" so bring it on. My classes started at eight o'clock in the morning. The ending times varied as some met several times a week and some only once. Rarely did they last past two-thirty or so, and Fridays there were no classes.

Surprisingly, I found myself enjoying the experience. For the first time that I could remember, I found learning fun. It was hard work but fun.

Part of our grade depended on class participation and participate I did. The ensuing discussions were often at odds with the instructor or others in class and lively debates were enjoyable.

Not all the courses were fun. Math was still a difficult challenge. Speech involved public speaking; something I found intimidating. Finding time to complete all the reading and work assignments was also a challenge. Term papers were a common assignment requiring hours in the library for the research. As I write this on a laptop computer that takes me anywhere I need to be at the push of a button, I think of how this would have made my life as a student easier. Hey, I did have a portable electric typewriter!

Before I knew it, the first semester was nearing the end and the dreaded final exams were looming. This would tell the story. Could I do this?

I knew that my grades were passing but were they good enough? I managed a Grade Point Average high enough to pass on to the next semester but it was closer than I would have liked. By the end of my freshman year I had managed a point accumulation of 2.8. Not great but I could keep going.

I had trouble with English Composition and caught the attention of the instructor.

Mr. Grieco told me he thought I had potential but not enough understanding on structure and organization. He told me that if I signed up for him next semester in a creative writing course, he would work with me and get my grade up. I did and he did.

I had to write a term paper on Catcher in the Rye . I turned in my first attempt and it bled red. He gave it back to me to redo after he explained what it needed and why. I came away from his class with 3.2 GPA for the term and a better understanding .on how to write a paper. It was to serve me well for the rest of my life and I never forgot his kindness.

All in all, the year went pretty well. I did well in some classes and not so well in others. I wanted to do better but learning how to learn takes time and I was working seven and a half hours every night at the Post Office and doing homework.

I had to be up early enough to make my eight o'clock classes. Thankful for the Fridays without classes and sometime between, I managed to get my reading and written assignments completed.

Time at home with the family was limited but we still did things together and visited with friends. There were always things that needed to be done around the house as well. Summer was over much too quickly and my second year at school would soon be starting.

I was too busy to worry much about my physical condition and was not really bothered by it. I was still able to do most everything I wanted to do. I would never be in an Ironman competition anyway. If I thought about the future, my concerns about what would happen to me in years to come would surface; so I simply stopped thinking about the future. Problem solved!

Once classes resumed, I quickly got back into the routine. I had several classes in my major this semester. One such class was engineering drafting.

I had become pretty good friends with one of the students in Industrial Arts. Bob Anglesea was in the drafting class with me as he was in most of the other ones. Class assignments involved taking an object and drawing it to engineering specifications. I like the class and enjoyed the mechanical drawing. The main problem was that the assignments were time sponges. A complex object could take several hours to reproduce on the drawing board. Bob lived only a few minutes away from the college and we would arrange to take our drawing tools and boards over to his house and work there when we had free time. His mom was great and always feeding us and fussing over us.

Once Maryrose returned to her teaching after maternity leave, money was a bit less of a worry. We certainly needed it as my college expenses were considerable and things like textbooks cost a fortune. Uncle Sam helped some with money from the GI bill but more was needed.

Now in my junior year, it looked like I might actually be able to complete college. The course work still had a number of subjects not related to my major. I had world geography, art, geology and geometry. In IA I had such courses as graphic arts, engine mechanics, ceramics, and woodworking.

Engine mechanics was a great course. We were to learn about the turbine-powered car that Chrysler Motors was involved with. They had a small fleet of the turbine driven cars out being tested in actual use. They had one brought in for us to inspect. It was pretty impressive.

Another engine that was unique was the "Wankel rotary engine." This employed a piston-less internal combustion engine that was small, had fewer moving parts and produced power at high rpm's. A Japanese car firm manufactured a car using this engine for a number of years.

There were times when some of us would get together and head down to the local pub for lunch and a brew. Sometimes we had a couple of hours before our next class.

I found that two or three mugs of beer did not improve the learning experience in my two o'clock world history class. Then, there was the mass lecture class in mythology. That was a most miserable course indeed.

At least one hundred students sat in an auditorium and listened to this professor talk about ancient gods and goddesses for an hour.

We were expected to write a term paper and pass the final exam based on our own notes. What notes? Miss a lecture and you were in trouble. I nearly failed this fool class. No way could I stay awake in it.

There were other areas of study that I had trouble with. Statistics was one of these. You had to come up with probability of events. This involved, for example, how many times the number six would come up when two dice were tossed one hundred times. Who cares? There were other subjects that were way more important to me.

As I was in a teachers preparation type of program, I had to get some practical experience actually teaching. Junior practicum as it was called had us going to a real school and paired with a working teacher. We were student teachers and expected to conduct classes under a professional teachers watchful eye.

This was what it was all about. My first class was mechanical drawing in a ninth grade class of about twenty students. I was to present the assignment, go over the methods and help them get started. I was pretty nervous at first but soon relaxed and started to enjoy it. They were a great class and cooperative for their age. I did well and finished the requirement with a glowing report.

Another requirement was to find an experience that served to mentor or somehow, assist someone who was in need. Some of us volunteered in hospitals or homes for the aged. I chose to volunteer at Overlook Hospital in the youth mental health care area.

They had a mentoring program that coupled an older big brother type with a troubled youth. We would be assigned a youngster that was being detained in the hospital for any number of reasons. We were to visit the patient twice a week and play games with them or go for walks or whatever. We just needed to be there for them for a little while. All of the patients were there for pretty serious problems.

I was assigned a young male of about ten years of age who had set several fires. One of his family members had been severely burned as a result. When I went there to visit him, I had to go through several locked doors to his ward. The doors were locked behind me. Not a good feeling. The patient was pretty normal as far as I could tell. We played games and talked and he seemed just fine. I never experienced any sort of issues for the entire semester while I did this mentoring. I do not know whatever became of him. I hoped he made a life for himself. As the semester end was getting close, it all changed.

Just as you figure that things are going pretty well it was inevitable that events would corner you into another quandary.

The Post Office where I worked decided that I must become a permanent employee as opposed to the temporary status. They were eliminating all temp positions. If I wanted to stay, I would be assigned to different hours that did not agree with my class schedule. This would mean I would have to reduce my class load to less than full time.

I had to maintain full time student status to get the government payments and I would miss graduating with my class. I had to fulfil senior student teacher requirements as well. Frustration hit me hard and I was about ready to just say to hell with it and quit. The family put a stop to this thinking quickly as they convinced me to hang in there. It was good advice.

I soon found a position with a company that provided computerized reservation services for various motels across the county. Motels had on-site terminals that they could record or receive reservations on and we maintained the database for a fee. Telamax was the name.

I worked with the huge Univac computers that were used back then. These computers were at least eight feet tall. I learned how to operate them, print out reports and many other tasks. The data storage system was punch cards, tape and big magnetic storage drums. They had to be maintained and I could work evenings. It did not pay as well as the Post Office but it was something and it allowed me to resume my intended class schedule.

Maryrose was by now, making pretty good money. We were not as cash strapped as before. No way could I have continued on without her. The boys were getting bigger now and a lot easier to be around for me. Diaper changing was rare duty.

My grades in school were getting progressively better too. My GPA was well over the 3.0 score. That was the equivalent of a B plus. I had little chance to be valedictorian but I was doing all right. It was about this time when I realized something pretty important.

From time to time I would find myself bemoaning my fate. As my condition continued to make itself known to me, I would grow despondent. I even announced at one point that when I became dependent on someone else that I would choose to find a permanent way out. I began to look around me and noticed that it was very common to find someone in a lot worse way than me.

The sight of a young child in a wheel chair being put on a store elevator was enough to bring tears. The struggle the gentleman who had somehow lost a leg had to endure just to board a bus struck me as heroic. The little girl down the street who had to shuffle along in leg braces showed me what real sacrifice was. Maybe one day I would be faced with this challenge too.

However, for now, I was in perfect health by comparison. I think it was at that time that I learned to accept my situation and was determined to pursue a more positive attitude. I was not always successful but it was a better attitude.

Our last semester before graduation was a busy one indeed. I carried a full class load of some fourteen credit hours and worked a full shift every night.

Eight o'clock classes were still the norm. We had more time off on certain days but the full days could last until four o'clock in the afternoon.

I was good friends with Bob Anglesea and Larry Mayo and we had some good times during the hours between some classes. Larry was a veteran of the Marine Corp. so was nearer my age. We would often head down to the local tavern for a sandwich and beer

Larry was married and had a couple of kids too. We eventually got our families together. Bob was still single and involved with his girlfriend who lived on the same street. It was good to have these friends and it helped us all to share in the difficulties of coping as students.

Nearing the day when commencement would arrive, we thought of where we would like to teach in our first jobs. We had finished our student teaching requirements and began the process of applying for teaching positions.

Some of our classmates had already gotten commitments for a contract. I applied to several school districts and landed a few interested schools.

The interview process was involved and we worried as to how to answer all the questions to their satisfaction. We were entitled to permanent teaching certificates for kindergarten through twelfth grade so could teach pretty much at any grade level.

Wyckoff Schools showed interest in me and they were closest to Hackensack out of the three or so schools that contacted me. An interview with the superintendent was arranged.

After a tense interview, I was offered a position of industrial arts teacher for the seventh and eighth grades at Eisenhower Junior High School.

They did not have a high school and the students were sent to another district after the eighth grade. There were actually two positions open and they asked me if I had any suggestions for the other slot. I thought of Bob and sure enough, he would start at the same time. We would be teaching together!

Meanwhile, I had to finish up classes, pass the final exams and prepare for commencement. A four year struggle was about to come to an end. All my hard work and sacrifice was going to pay off. I still, to this day, marvel at the achievement.

It was Spring of 1970. The commencement would take place in the Giant's stadium where the two thousand or so graduates would have room. We were in our cap and gowns and I joined in the procession to receive my Bachelor of Arts degree in Education. There was much celebration afterwards and I was pretty proud of myself. A true milestone.

That summer I was to travel out to Omaha, Nebraska for Telamax. Several crews were to take a rented truck and deliver computer terminals all across states such as Pennsylvania, Ohio, Indiana and Illinois. They had a customer service center in Omaha to serve all of these terminals and I was given the task of training the agents. It was a fun job and satisfied my need to travel as I had the same wanderlust that my father had.

By the time September rolled around, I was ready for my first year as a professional educator. Or, so I thought.

Around the time school was to open, all of the new teachers were invited to a luncheon at a nearby restaurant. This was a time to meet the others and get acquainted. There were eleven of us including my friend Bob. It was a pleasant experience and made our entry to the school system a bit easier.

My beginning salary was over nine thousand dollars a year! This was pretty good money in 1970, at least for teachers. It was the most I had ever earned before so I was content. My medical insurance and life insurance were paid for. Things were pretty good and the future was promising.

We were essentially on probation as teachers for the first three years. We had class observations several times throughout the year by the principal. We were expected to prepare and submit our lesson plans for each class. I taught mechanical drawing, wood shop, and metal shop. These were the traditional courses that had been part of the curriculum for a long time.

There was a new emphasis in education about to take place. Bob and I would be charged with curriculum development that supposedly would prepare our students better for their years to come. The other classes would be changing too.

The latest concept that was to take hold was the "team teaching" movement. Students were grouped into teams together and taught by the same teachers every day. Teachers had the same students for the same class every day.

Industrial Arts and other electives would continue the same way but we had to develop new curriculum. It was believed that the old shop courses were no longer relevant. Students were not to be prepared to work in the trades. They would likely go on to college and enter the professions. Why waste their time with wood shop or drafting that they would never use? I did not buy into it then and I do not today.

There is a life-long purpose to experiencing hands-on work with basic materials that we need to have in our lives.

Just ask the young person next to you today to measure a length of board to the nearest one sixteenth of an inch and watch the blank expression on his or her face! However, we had no choice in the matter and came up with a program that was accepted as state of the art at that time. Bob and I would be team-teaching a brand new concept.

The teaching program was entitled "The Wonderful World of Manufacturing". In brief, the idea was to break the classes up into small groups that would be responsible for different parts of the manufacturing process. No one student would complete a project but rather it would be a group effort.

You had the design group that came up with the ideas, the planners, the assembly lines and the final inspections. We would select a project such as a screwdriver and put it into production from start to finish! That particular project received less than stellar reviews as the finished screwdrivers were used throughout the school to dismantle radiator covers or anything else held together with screws! It was a grand idea in theory but I am still of the opinion that the old traditional ways have more value.

It was around 1971 that I was asked to volunteer to go into the hospital for some research testing. I was asked to submit to a battery of tests that would help the doctors to better understand the muscular dystrophy structure.

As I recall, it was scheduled during summer vacation. For the better part of two weeks, I would be subjected to all kinds of tests. Maryrose took me across the George Washington bridge and I was processed into Columbia Presbyterian Hospital's neurology suite.

I was to get another muscle biopsy in the right shoulder. This one I was not awake for. Each day I was scheduled for different tests. Electroshock studies were not much fun. Needles were inserted in various muscle groups and subjected to electrical charges. This would cause contractions and were very uncomfortable. There were other tests and long discussions concerning my father and grandfather.

The doctor in charge was pretty critical of Maryrose's pregnancy. Of course, it was way too late for that concern at this point. It was confirmed to me that this disease was inherited, my father had it and so did my grandfather. Each of us was affected in different ways.

It is accepted that approximately fifty percent of offspring will be affected. It seemed to me to be more likely to affect males than females. Now, it is known that it affects both sexes equally.

Many factors came into play as to the severity of the affliction. There seemed to be no way to predict what would happen. I have carried around a lot of guilt over the years once I learned that two of my children would have to and are dealing with this FSHD.

Craig, my oldest, seemed not to be affected. Scott, as the second oldest was definitely affected and so was my future third son, Todd. Deanna yet to be born would be without obvious symptoms. What a terrible legacy to leave to your offspring. I hoped and prayed that the day would come when a cure will be there for them. For all of us!

I was profoundly affected by all of this and it changed me in certain ways that I did not fully understand at the time.

As the both of Maryrose and I had been teaching up until this last pregnancy, we usually were able to go places in the summer time. That summer in August, we welcomed Todd Gregory into the family. We stayed pretty close to home that summer. I now had three sons so the Higgins name was safe for another generation!

I was pretty content with going hunting with Alan and learning about the upland game style. In Kansas or Nebraska, you would simply walk the fields to the fence line and the pheasant would take to the air.

Here in New Jersey, there were lots of places to hunt and lots of places for the game to hide. Old farms were common and the woods were everywhere.

Most people in the Midwest or west assume New Jersey is one big city but there is a lot of open land. You had your choice of stocked pheasants or the native ruffed grouse. Stocked pheasants did not react the same as their Midwest cousins, they were almost too easy as they would not fly unless you almost stepped on them. Bird dogs were most useful for this type of hunting.

The grouse were another thing altogether. They hung out in the thickest bushes or most inaccessible bogs and only flew after you passed them! Usually, they scared the heck out of you! Then there was the Timber-doodle!

The Woodcock is an east coast migratory bird about the size of a pigeon. It was fast and had the ability to hover much like a hummingbird does. It rarely offered you any decent shot and misses were the norm. Still, it was a lot of fun and I truly enjoyed being out in the woods. It was not all that important if we bagged anything or not.

It was inevitable that I would start thinking about getting my own bird dog. I had hunted over a pair of my friend's dogs and it was much more productive.

The dogs would range out in front until they caught a scent. It was neat watching them slowly advance on the bird, stop, tail out and front paw in the air. If the bird moved, they would stay with it. They knew enough to keep a fifteen or twenty foot distance away until you released them.

These were Brittany Spaniels and were flushing dogs. Once released, they would rush in and make the birds fly. They would retrieve the fallen bird if you brought one down. Their expressions when you missed were definitely ones of disapproval!

This same friend came across an English setter that was looking for a home. She was only about six months old and should be at a good age for training. Her name was Turn-Hi-Gemini on her papers but we just called her Gemi...most of the time.

As it turned out, the dog was as dumb as a post! The only thing she pointed at were butterflies! When out in the field, she just ran! Everywhere! When called, she ran faster! The only birds she ever kicked up were the ones she ran over and they flew in panic!

Now, I admit, this was my first dog ever and dog training was not part of my experience. I had read everything I could get my hands on about how to train a bird dog. Had I spent the money on a professional trainer instead of all the books I bought, I might have had a chance!

According to the books, there was nothing to it. You showed the dog what you wanted it to do and repeat as necessary. Before you know it, the dog is miraculously pointing out game and all is as it should be.

Hell, I could not get Gemi's attention long enough to issue a command, much less repeat as necessary!

No one would go hunting with me if I had Gemi with me. I guess butterflies were not high on their game list. I soon gave up the hope of ever having a faithful four-legged hunting partner and left her home.

I soon was hearing reports from Maryrose's grandmother that Gemi was raiding her goody stash. She kept various snacks next to her chair in the living room where she watched TV. There were many other instances where Gemi did not endear herself to the family.

Soon, she was banned to the basement. This was not fair to her so we finally were able to find her a home on a farm where she could point out butterflies all day long!

Several years later, our next dog would be a Yorkshire terrier named Sir Dust Mop! At least Dusty did not bother butterflies. His goal in life was to offend my oldest son, Craig! That proved to be easily accomplished!

The year 1972 would soon be over and so would my third decade. For the most part, it was a good time in my life. I had accomplished much and had much to look forward to. I had three fine sons, made it through school and made the decision to continue on and get a Master's degree in Education. Life was indeed good.

CHAPTER 4

Going to college at night was somewhat tedious. I was up early in the morning, taught classes all day and had to make it over to East Orange to the Seton Hall University campus. This university was a private Catholic school.

This was another new experience. For the first time, I had professors that were priests. One such instructor was a real character. Most of the classes were attended by males and females. This guy came in and looked around carefully at each of us and then asked, "Are there any undercover nuns in this class?"

Some of the instructors were contracted from the outside. I had a class with one that decreed that no one was likely to earn an A in his class. An A was a perfect grade and no one was perfect so do not expect it. He was right. I received my only two B's from him out of the entire thirty-seven credits I earned. All the rest of my grades were four zero or straight A's . Even stranger, my term paper that I submitted was noted as one of the best he had ever read! Go figure!

Graduate studies were not terribly difficult, just time intensive. The only time I was pretty up tight was when we were scheduled for the comprehensive tests.

You could avoid the comps if you chose to write a thesis. I figured this to be way too much time and work so I selected the comps. This was an exam on a variety of topics we had studied over the past two years that would take several hours. It was pass or fail.

If you failed, you started all over again on the entire program! Scary! I soon found out that I was successful and would be eligible to receive my Master of Arts in Education. I was also permanently certified to be an administrator in any public school system. Of course, I was never political enough to ever be considered for that position.

The boys were getting older and bigger. Little league baseball, cub scouts and assorted other activities kept us all busy. With finances under better control, we were starting to consider traveling some more. I still felt the urge now and then, to see some new country. I bought a used tent trailer and we made a few close by trips camping. Everyone seemed to enjoy the experience. The little tent trailer was surprisingly roomy once it was set up. It was off the ground and cozy on chilly nights. Closed up, it was easy to tow and store.

I saw a few truck campers that caught my eye. They were pretty comfortable with tiny kitchens and even a portable toilet. I started looking into these and found that there were kits available to build your own.

I ordered the plans and was soon engaged in building the sides, roof and ends. The floor area would fit in a standard eight-foot pickup bed. There was a large bunk over the cab area and the dinette converted to a double bed.

When on my own time, I would build a section in the school shop and when completed, take it home. I had use of a single car garage and began assembly there. I owned a used Ford pickup that I drove at the time.

When I had the basic shell assembled, I purchased the aluminum siding kit and proceeded to cover the entire camper with a two-color prefinished skin.

The roof was a galvanized metal sheet that was coated with a tar-like material to waterproof everything. It also had a couple of roof vents that could be opened.

The window kit gave plenty of natural lighting and ventilation all around the camper. Soon, I was ready to start the interior.

I put in a small refrigerator that worked off of standard AC voltage or the twelve-volt car system. The stove was a three burner compact unit with a tiny oven that was propane fired. I had a water tank and a small sink with running water.

All in all, it was a neat, self-contained little home on wheels! It took several months to complete but was soon ready for its first trip.

It turned out to be a well-used part of my life. It had a three-jack system that allowed me to raise it off the bed of the truck enough to drive out from under it so I did not have to carry it around when not in use. The total cost was a fraction of what a factory unit would have cost so I was well satisfied and took considerable pride in it.

This truck camper was taken on several cross-country trips. The longest trip was the trek out to the farm. We went with some friends that had a trailer.

My youngest son, Todd, would celebrate his first birthday on this trip. Aunt Dorothy and (now) Uncle Dale were great hosts. They were now living in a newer and more complete farm setting a bit southwest of the original home place. Here they had amenities that the old place lacked: indoor plumbing, a large barn, outbuildings for the implements, and the livestock were just a few of the improvements. The original farm was now well over two thousand acres with about two thirds of it tillable.

There were cattle that provided milk which was sold but was also available to drink. It is worth mentioning that this milk was to die for. So rich and tasty! The kids had a great time and I think everyone else enjoyed the experience as well.

Another trip was a chuck-hunting trip to Ohio with Bob with the new varmint rifles we had built, hunting trips up to New York State and others. The camper was well used.

There was another trip worth special notice. The boys, Maryrose and I decided to go to Assateague Island in Virginia to see the wild ponies and the round up. Maryrose's cousin, Mary Ellen, came with us as well. I thought of this place as I remembered it as a kid, from reading the book, Misty of Chincoteague[1]. Each year they rounded up the ponies and a few of the foals are offered up for adoption after very careful screening of the potential owner. This kept the size of the herd small enough for the land they roam. I figured this would be a great experience for us so off we went.

It is worth noting that Mary Ellen was not what you would describe as a seasoned camper! In fact, Chincoteague was likely the farthest she had ever been from New Jersey in her life!

She was game though and provided the rest of us with many laughs. Once camp was set up and we settled in, we decided to go crabbing. We were camped within a short walking distance to the waterway that held plenty of crabs. Maryrose was the only one who knew what to do.

The idea was to take a string and tie it around a piece of chicken, preferably after it had been in the sun for a while. You drop it in the water and wait a bit.

[1]Marguerite Henry, Misty of Chincoteague, Rand Mc Nally, Chicago, Ill, 1947.

1

A long handled net at the ready; you would carefully pull the string up until you could see the piece of chicken and quite often, a crab. He would hang on to his "lunch" hopefully long enough for you to get the net under him and he became lunch!

The next scene involved Maryrose and Mary Ellen putting on a pot of water to boil on our tiny camper kitchen stove. The bucket of crabs was then transferred to the boiling water for cooking. Somehow, Mary Ellen managed to drop one on the floor of the camper while still very much alive! The ensuing panic was a site to behold as the two adult females vacated the camper in record time! I think I hurt myself from laughing so hard!

The town of Chincoteague celebrated the pony round up every year. Local vendors and musicians were all up and down the street. For a dollar or so, you could get a fried oyster sandwich that was delicious.

The town held a raffle for several prizes that you could buy tickets for. This year, they had a drawing for a seventeen-foot camper trailer as the biggest prize. I bought ten dollars' worth and forgot about it after filling in the details. You did not have to be present to win.

A bit later, after we had returned home we got a phone call from the island. I had won the trailer! My ticket won! That was pretty exciting. I think that was the one and only thing of significance that I ever won.

I soon sold the truck camper and we bought a station wagon with a towing package so there was room for all. There cannot be any passengers in a towed trailer like we were able to do with the truck camper.

There were a number of advantages the trailer had over the truck camper. It had more room, a bigger kitchen and more sleeping areas. When we got to our destination, it was a simple matter to unhitch and you had your car at your disposal. Towing was not difficult.

The Oldsmobile station wagon handled the trailer pretty well. Mileage was not great but gas was reasonable. The truck had done no better. The next summer, we loaded up and headed for our next adventure.

As much as I wanted to ignore the signs, it was become more evident that my body was under attack. My right arm was diminished in an apparent way. The triceps muscle had shrunk considerably. It was not as bad with the left arm. The effect was a reduction in pushing strength and the ability to do things over my head. Other than that, I did not notice much obvious impairment.

One more thing; my ability to whistle was pretty much gone! Now, I had never really given it much thought. Whistling was not something I engaged in much anyway. Funny though, when you cannot do it anymore, you miss it! I would find myself testing it for some time to come!

This summer was probably 1974. We packed the trailer up and headed for Disneyworld in Florida. We had reservations for the campground that was right on the park. Todd was still pretty young. The other two were pretty excited though.

Craig had managed to earn a cast on his forearm that would be due to be removed while we were away. No problem "doctor" Curt would remove it when the time came. Those casts are not so easy to remove as one would think. It took me a while but was finally successful! I even managed to save his arm from further harm! Disneyworld was great. We all had a great time. I went on many of the rides with the boys. Space Mountain was pretty neat. They had a submarine ride that was cool as well. The haunted house was very well done.

The campsite was really nice and there was many things to keep the kids occupied. We also took several daytrips to other area attractions such as Sea World and an alligator farm where some guy wrestled with a huge alligator! Soon, our time was up and the next leg of the adventure was to drive in a northwest direction towards the farm in Nebraska.

We ended up in Nashville, Tennessee and saw the "Grand Ole Opry". We went through at least six different states from Florida to get to the farm. Each day we would try to find a campground to stop at around three or so to take advantage of the swimming pool and just to kick back and relax from driving all day.

The boys would head for the pinball machines with a fist full of quarters. I, a cold beer and maybe a quick swim and all was well. We would fix a simple dinner and sit around an open fire. It was a good time and a real time. The next morning, we would get up early and be on our way by seven or so. After several days of this, we arrived in Rushville, Nebraska.

The farm was always a great place to visit. The kids had a lot of fun with the animals and the vehicles like the Trackster which Uncle Dale used in the winter to take hay to the cattle. It was a small track-driven vehicle that could go most anywhere. It was great fun to drive.

By now, Uncle Dale had acquired a new tractor. The thing was a behemoth with four tires taller than a man. It was four-wheel drive with an enclosed air-conditioned cab complete with radio. You sat up high and could see all around you. I learned to drive it and did some summer fallow work for old time's sake! It was a huge improvement over the old Case tractor.

After a too short time, we headed home. We went up a bit north to the Black Hills region and saw Mount Rushmore before proceeding east. The badlands and a few of the typical tourist traps rounded out the adventure. The herds of buffalo and antelope were things that may never be seen again.

One highlight was the arrival in Baxter, Iowa...my great grandfather's past home so long ago! Not much there that was noteworthy but at least, I had been there and so had three of my children.

It was back to the routine of teaching and dealing with every day issues. We wanted to get a home of our own. Maryrose and I went around a few different areas to price and look at various homes for sale.

Our friends, Mary and Alan had a home in Oakland so we looked up that way. Everything seemed to be beyond our means though. We had not saved enough to put down an adequate down payment and the monthly payments were pretty high.

Maryrose's parents told her that if we wanted to build a house, they would give us the back lot behind their house. It was a lot about fifty by one hundred feet. With the land equity, we could afford to build.

I found a contractor and plans for a house that we both felt was a good choice and proceeded to make it happen. A short time later, we had a two-story house with three bedrooms, two baths, family room with fireplace and a one-car garage. It was not fancy but suited our needs very well. I was not very pleased that we ended up here as I had envisioned moving away from the Hackensack area but admitted that the compromise was to our advantage. Now, all we had to do was pay for it!

Frankly, I was growing more despondent each day. My arm strength was slipping away. I could not even lift a pillow straight up over my head! Some of this carried over into my home life and work. I kept telling myself it was not so bad. I could still do most of what I needed to do but it was worrisome nonetheless. I know I was drinking too much. That was a trap so easily fallen into. It gave temporary relief to forget the problem. Of course, it was still there the next morning. I wish I could say that I was able to overcome all this and move on. That would take more time.

Teaching was changing almost every year. It seemed that no one really understood the direction Industrial Arts should take. The old traditions were slowly being cast aside; boys took shop and girls were in home economics. That premise was no longer so.

We had to develop curriculum that included both sexes. New technologies were introduced. I set up courses in photography and electronics. We still kept basic drafting. These were somewhat successful, at least for a few.

Sometimes, it seemed that we were only keeping them busy without thought to actual purpose. Many students came to me in drafting but could not understand simple fractions! They could not read a ruler! What were they doing in their math class?

By now, it is in the later 70's. Citizen Band radios were the rage. Everyone had one in their car! Looking back on it, it was pretty silly. Still, we had great fun talking the talk! Hunting was still part of my activities.

By now, my teaching partner, Bob Anglesea had taken up hunting and shooting as well. He then proceeded to obtain a huge collection of various weapons. I was never sure just why he wanted them all but collect them he did. Me, I had my shotgun and a single handgun.

I also had the varmint rifle that I built from scratch, that is, the Mauser action in 22-250 caliber that I bedded in a hand-crafted English walnut stock. The stock was carved out after many long hours with chisel and files. Sanding and checkering of the forearm and stock was completed. The addition of a telescope sight and look out woodchucks!

I have always enjoyed working with my hands. I loved working with wood especially. In college, we were given some basics but only time and effort makes one proficient. I learned a lot from Bob as he had actually worked in a cabinet shop and thus knew a lot more than I did. Once I grasped the concept of accuracy, I became much better.

Furniture, for example, is basically a box or a combination of boxes. If you can build a box, you can make most anything!

A box has four sides. Two of the sides must be exactly the same length and width as do the other two sides. If not, it is not square and the assembly will fail. End of lesson. I made a number of items such as end tables and a platform bed. I also made a bar for our family room and a number of other projects.

In September of 1978, Deanna Dorothy was born. She was my one and only daughter. She was a beautiful baby, albeit, a bit of a surprise! I had sort of figured that we were finished with baby rearing. Please, no more diapers! Oh well, move on.

This was not a real good time in my life. I began to feel closed in. Too much was affecting me and I was restless. The work at school was starting to wear on me. The teaching part was fine but the constant requirements for change and the difficulty with some of the problem kids was beginning to take its toll.

If you sent a discipline problem to the office, it simply came back that you were at fault. Parents complained about everything and were heard. The professional teacher was not given consideration. 1979 saw me ready for change.

My marriage was not doing well, I was not doing well. I still drank too much. I am not real proud of this period of my life.

In 1980, the school system was going through serious budget issues and many staff were to be terminated. Industrial Arts would be reduced to one teacher. My military service gave me an edge and I would be the one to stay. However, with my state of mind at the time, I decided that if I could qualify for a disability pension, I would give up the position.

It was becoming an issue with me working with some of the machines in the shop such as the table saw, etc. I could still operate them but only if I did so my own way. It was not the correct way to teach an operation.

I applied to the state for disability retirement and it was finally accepted. I left teaching in nineteen eighty but did not officially retire until February 1981 due to accumulated benefits. I had taught nearly eleven years in public schools and it was now time to move on. This was not received well on the home front either. The family was upset with me as well.

I soon found work as a field technician for a copier company. I did not realize it at the time but that business is only slightly above vacuum cleaner sales and service! Still, while the pay was pretty low we got a new car that was paid for and they provided the tools. I kind of liked working out in the field. I attended several training classes on the copiers and while they were pretty sophisticated, they were pretty easy to service and repair. Most of the work was simple preventative maintenance.

It was at this job that I was to meet Laura. She worked up in the front office and I did not have much contact with her. In fact, for quite a while, there was virtually no contact. Laura being Laura started saying good morning to me the few times our paths crossed and I responded in kind.

I often worked in the field on day trips that would take me to Long Island and Manhattan but the few times I was back in the office before closing, I would venture over to a local pub for a beer or two. Laura happened to show up there one of these times. We became friendly and it evolved into a comfortable routine. We would sometimes go for lunch together or for drinks at the pub and the friendship seemed to grow.

Things were no better at home now. I made up my mind that life was much too short to settle for a situation that was not going well. I decided to leave and file for divorce based on non-compatibility.

I truly felt bad for the kids but what I was currently offering could not have been the best for them. I was sure the tension and fighting could not be a very healthy atmosphere for them. Just to add fuel to the fire, I lost my license due to an accident and DUI charge. This was an expensive and drawn out incident. It actually took many weeks for the day in court and the sentencing. In the meantime, a lot had happened. The copier job would soon be history. I had issues with the boss and his offensive girlfriend and I would soon be without a license so I left.

I left the house too. It was time to start over. This was truly a low point in my life and I would never want to relive it again. It is painful just to write about and I am certainly not proud of the time. Life just had to get better.

A night or two in a cheap hotel forced me to review my options and I began the search for an apartment. I stayed with Laura and her Mom in Ridgefield for a short time until I could secure a place to live. I had a few dollars that I had squirreled away and found an apartment in a two-family house in nearby Lodi. It was small and simple but cozy and did not cost too much for rent. I did not have any furniture and bought a mattress to put on the floor and have a place to sleep!

Parking was another problem as the street was often crowded with cars. Laura moved in to the apartment with me and we started a new life together.

Laura helped me out a lot during this difficult time. I had no job and was without a car for now. Laura ferried me around for some time until I managed to get back my license and get another vehicle. Hopefully, I would soon get back my self-esteem as well. After a couple of months without a license, it was time to get some new transportation. I found a black Ford pickup in great condition for a reasonable price. Laura no longer had to provide taxi service to get me to and from work.

I had found a job not too far from where we lived that suited me well. The company was a manufacturing and research facility that specialized in glass bead manufacturing for highway safety products. The reflective qualities of the painted stripes on most highways and the reflective markers alongside of the road are due to the embedded tiny beads of glass..

On the premises were several massive furnaces that broken recycled glass was fed into and melted. Air was used to blow against the molten glass and the results were millions of tiny glass beads. They would be sifted and sorted into different sizes and then packaged up for sale.

My job was as an engineering technician. The professional engineers would come up with ideas to improve process or other new innovations and I would be tasked to build a prototype of their ideas.

Often, I would only get a simple sketch and a verbal description to build some contraption. It was up to me to put it together. I had a pretty nice work area and plenty of supplies. Most of the projects involved machining or welding.

Welding was not a skill I was great at. I got permission to take a class in welding at night school and that helped a lot. I really enjoyed the job. I was left pretty much alone and no two jobs were ever the same. It suited me.

My oldest son came to work for them in the summer. When he finished school, he was still with them. Craig worked for them for quite some time. I had this urge to get away from this part of the country. That wanderlust passed on to me by my father seemed to be calling.

Laura and I were having a grand old time setting up a home and getting to know each other. She added one very large cat to the scene. Bebes was a big old black and white tomcat that she had adopted and there was no way she was going to give him up.

I was warned not to yell or correct him in any way until he got to know and accept me. No cat is going to dictate terms to me! I chased him off the counter...he left a wet calling card in my briefcase! I pushed him off the table...I got a wet shoe! I left him alone and he used his litter box!

We had an understanding. We soon became good buddies. Go figure. Things were going along pretty well. That February, 1982 was the end of another decade. I was forty years old.

Chapter Five

Laura and I began talking about getting out of New Jersey and finding a new life out in the Midwest. We figured we could use the farm as our starting point. Aunt Dorothy and Uncle Dale were okay with the plan.

We decided to buy a used tent camper and managed to sell off most of the few furnishings we had. We then packed up what we would need and having given job notices and said our goodbyes, we were ready. I am sure Laura was having some concerns about leaving her Mom as I was about leaving my kids but we were committed

The loaded pickup and camper were ready. We hoisted the big cat into the cab thus putting the Ford near its weight limits, and we were off! This was August 1983.

We took our time and stopped when tired and set up camp. Bebes was confined to the tent camper but was pretty much out of it due to the tranquilizers we had given him. He never was really happy riding in a vehicle and would meow constantly. The meds helped some.

After a couple of days, we set up camp in Illinois near Chicago. Somehow, the fool cat escaped from the camper and Laura was frantic trying to find him.

I figured we had lost him but no, Laura wandered around the campground shouting his name and rattling his cat treats.

Darned if she did not find him! Anything to do with his food would always do the trick!

We traveled across Iowa and the gazillion acres of cornfields and on into Nebraska. Quite a few hours later, we made it to the farm. My aunt and uncle met Laura and they hit it off right away. We were tired but excited and looking forward to finding work and a new home.

We rested for a few days and Laura got to know the farm better. We went to the old homestead a bit northeast of Uncle Dale's farm. He still worked the land but the old place was used more for storage or occasionally, the house was rented out.

Laura loved the farm animals! The cattle became instant pets. The infinite number of cats that were more or less feral gave her pause. They did not take to being picked up and ran in every direction when she tried. The farm dog, Ivy, was friendly though and enjoyed her fussing over her. There were chickens and hogs and a horse as I recall which all became potential pets as well. If we stayed long enough, she would give names to every one of them!

Uncle Dale gave me some space in the machine shed and I offloaded some of the tools that I had kept and brought with me. We stayed in the tent camper at night because of the cat. Aunt Dorothy prepared her usual simple but great meals so we ate well.

We then proceeded to look for gainful employment. Both of us were willing to do pretty much anything that would provide income. It soon became very apparent that this was not going to be easy. There were no jobs anywhere near.

Rushville was shrinking and many stores and businesses had disappeared. There was no manufacturing. It was not promising. Uncle Dale gave me some work on the farm but they could not afford a fulltime hand. I worked the tractor doing my favorite thing...summer fallow! Laura check the local newspapers to no avail. We had to do something. Our savings would not last forever. Besides, it was starting to get cold. A tent trailer is definitely not suited to Nebraska winters! We made the decision to go on up to Chadron, Nebraska.

This was a much larger town and even boasted a small college. Surely, we would find something there. We rented a stationary trailer that was roomy and pretty comfortable near the edge of town. Money was beginning to be a real concern. We started looking for work right away. Chadron had a state unemployment office and we went there nearly every day.

There was nothing to be had. I could not even get a job as a highway flagman or filling station attendant. Laura applied where she could for any kind of secretarial work and met with the same results, nothing. My teaching credentials were worthless. The Master's degree was again useless.

Our friends from New Jersey, Annie and Paul were due to arrive in Nebraska in a few days. Paul was an owner/operator of a long distance moving rig. He owned an over the road tractor and hauled for a major moving company. Annie often drove with him and they were bringing out some of the things we had left behind in New Jersey. We were to meet with them at a rest stop on Interstate Eighty and pick up the items. We made the rendezvous and had a great visit. It was really good to meet some friendly faces for a time.

Our time together was way too short. Annie told us that when we were ready to come back, they would take us in until we could get settled. I think that started the thinking that returning was not too bad an idea. Still, my stubborn will kept saying that we would keep trying for a bit longer.

Another setback was the date of the final divorce from Maryrose. I had to appear in court to hear the final decree. It was decided that I would fly back and get it over with. Laura would remain in Chadron.

I got on a plane in Chadron that went to Denver. It was a very small turboprop aircraft. In Denver, I got on a regular carrier into Newark, New Jersey. There I rented a car and headed for the courthouse. Soon, it was over and I reversed the trip to get back to Chadron. I did not waste any time visiting and just wanted to get back to Laura. It was not a fun trip.

We were not getting anywhere in Chadron and it was decided that maybe we should try further west or south. We were not far from Lusk, Wyoming and headed for there. We stopped in Casper and had the same result...nothing. There simply was no work to be had in the entire area. The next stop was Denver. Our thinking was that a big city like Denver should be much easier to find work.

The drive to Colorado was not all dismal. Laura and I got to see a lot of new country and we had a lot of fun as we drove from place to place. I have more than a few happy memories of that time!

Once in Denver, I called my half-brother Greg and told him we were in town. We were directed to his home and the reunion was great. Greg and I were pretty much strangers but we had a lot in common and were soon at ease with each other. Our first night there, we woke up to nearly a foot of snow! Denver weather was strange. By the next day, it was melted and gone!

We stayed long enough to determine that the job offerings there were not very good either. Greg thought he might get me a job in construction as he was a field superintendent of a heavy equipment company. I only had to learn how to operate a bulldozer! I actually went to work with him one day and he showed me the ropes. Kind of reminded me of the summer fallow work!

By this time, it was looking pretty obvious that we should probably just give the whole idea up. Laura was missing her family and I was more than a little discouraged. This whole part of the country was obviously suffering severe hardships with almost no growth. We finally called Annie and Paul and told them we would be coming back.

We drove back to Chadron, packed up and stopped by the farm to pick up some things. We bought a used compact Oldsmobile Starfire that was a pretty good deal. Turns out that Laura soon hated it. It was stick shift and she did not like driving it. Still, we would need two vehicles upon our return. Bag and baggage, we headed for New Jersey after saying our goodbyes once again.

I had mixed feelings about this as I felt the failure and disappointment. I knew that I would never have another chance. Laura was absolutely wonderful about all this. I know she was anxious to get home to her Mom but she really tried to make this work and I was really proud of her. She was by my side through the whole ordeal.

Steady work for us would be available back in New Jersey. There was far greater opportunity. Perhaps this was true in other parts of the country as well but the east was a logical choice because of our families. When we began our return, we drove up to Interstate 90 and proceeded east.

On our way we passed through the Pine Ridge Indian reservation which had been in the national news from time to time. It is noteworthy to mention that it was obviously a very depressed area. Jobs were non-existent and the Indian survived only because of subsidized government care. It seemed a very sad end for a once proud people.

Once again, on our way up to Rapid City, we were to see herds of bison. They had made a remarkable recovery and there were many around the area. We did not linger in Rapid City. We had tried there earlier and the job situation was no better.

We turned east and proceeded on our way home. There was much to see as we began our trek east. The Badlands were a sight to behold. I had seen them several times before. They are very widespread with a lot of history for years gone by.

We stopped in Wall, South Dakota and visited the famous drugstore there. It is a typical Midwestern town that just happens to have this huge store that sells just about everything one could imagine.

After that, there was not much to see except prairie and ranches for the next few hundred miles. We learned that buffalo were being raised by some of the ranches as an alternative to beef cows.

If memory serves me, I think we drove south out of Sioux Falls towards Omaha, Nebraska where we took Interstate 80 on east. Just past Omaha, we were in Iowa and the endless cornfields.

A ways outside of De Moines we would take a brief jump of a few miles north to Baxter, Iowa where my great grandfather had once lived long ago! Soon, we were once again heading eastward. Several days later, the Delaware Water Gap was before us and we were almost back to where we had started nearly three months ago!

We arrived back in Lodi, New Jersey where Annie and Paul Fagan awaited us. It was a great reunion and we were happy to be back. It was then, that our dear friends showed us to our guest quarters. Annie had decorated the basement of the house with furnishings and drapes. It was cozy and attractive. We had a short-term place to stay! What a surprise! It gave us time to find work and locate a place to live. To say we were grateful would be an understatement.

Laura was rehired by her previous employer, Falcon Jet Corp. They had not yet hired a person for her job after she had previously left! It was a good break for us.

I eventually was hired by a Canadian based company name Bonaire. They manufactured consumer products having to do with air purification and needed a person to handle setting up the servicing of their products in the U.S.

It was my primary function to select, train and oversee the independent contractors with the day-to-day repairs of our product. For the most part, these service centers were already in existence and serviced many other products. They simply added our product line to their list. .

I traveled all over the United States selecting and getting the servicing operational. I would go out for a couple of weeks at a time and went as far as Alaska to get these facilities on board. I enjoyed the job and the travel.

At some point it was decided that Laura and I would get married. I certainly did not oppose this but I am not sure I had given it much previous thought. We were settled in and both were working so it was going pretty well for us. We did need to find our own place soon.

Annie and Laura were soon busy planning our simple nuptials. They decided they would bake a wedding cake and we would have a celebration at home in Lodi after the vows. The day arrived and all went well. Laura's brother served as my best man and Annie witnessed Laura. Paul was on a trip. Everything went smoothly and we were now man and wife. Sometimes, even I made good decisions!

We soon found a place nearby in Garfield that suited us. The second story apartment was large and comfortable. The main problem was parking. We had to find two spots on the street for the cars and that was difficult. When it snowed, it was a nightmare!

Still, we made do and were pretty happy. The Spring of 1984 found us on a weekend visit up to Passaic county.

On a whim, we drove up and stopped into a real estate office in West Milford, NJ. This was pretty far up north close to the NY border. Not expecting much, the agent that finally assisted us spoke of a newly available property up the mountain and urged us to take a look at it before it was actually listed. We piled into his car and he took us to this small little ranch a few miles away. The owner was a recent widow and wanted to sell and move away to be with her family.

The house was essentially a summer home that had been converted to year around living. It was far from fancy and needed much work but we both took a liking to it. The sloped property was protected by many trees and the dirt road was in fair shape. There were no other immediate homes within site of the house and that appealed to us. Also, no more parking problems!

We did not have any money saved up worth mentioning and explained that to Mike, the agent. He thought we could probably get approved with just a few thousand dollars. We talked it over and made an offer. The owner was asking for sixty five thousand and we offered sixty. She came back with sixty-two thousand and we accepted! Between our meager savings and our credit card, we were able to scrape up the minimum down payment! We were now new homeowners!

We closed in June, 1984. The commute was easy for me but Laura had a longer trip to work. This would soon change for her. In the meantime, we began work on our new very old home!

This house was built by hand about 1947. Many of the materials were used and from an old factory in Paterson, New Jersey. It was built well enough and quite strong but there were some annoying issues that had to be overcome.

For example, some of the wall studs were real two by fours made in a time before modern mill methods. They are rough and not at all like the modern two by four. Today's stud is milled and considerable less than an actual two by four dimension.

The builder/home owner used new studs when he ran short of the old used ones. The result was walls that undulated down their length! That half-inch difference made for a poor surface to attach sheetrock panels to!

Rooms would be disassembled and rebuilt using modern studs and new sheetrock. This was a long term project and we both learned on the job! We move doors, windows and walls as we proceeded. It was time and labor intensive but we were able to make it ours and it was cozy and comfortable. The house that I had built in Hackensack was new and never needed anything other than routine maintenance. This old house was like a long-term hobby to rebuild it to our needs and likes. It was a lot more fun than when I built the new house!

It was difficult for me to perform work over my head. My upper arms would not support a hammer. I managed by using two hands even though starting a nail was difficult. I discovered that screws were much easier for me to use. With the new cordless tools coming out it became routine to replace nailing with screws. I also discovered pneumatic nail guns that made it easier to install trim pieces and hold work in place..

As I continued to grow weaker, I learned new and different ways to accomplish the same job. It might well take longer but it was done and done well. Learning to live with muscle mass disappearing is a process of compromise and adaptation.

There almost always is another way to do the same task or solve the problem at hand. In a sense, one becomes an inventor on the fly! It would have been easy to become frustrated and overwhelmed with despair, but to what end? I often reminded myself that many others fought a much tougher battle! With Laura at my side, we managed quite well.

It was not long before Laura started talking about a dog.. She was fond of Springer Spaniels and had owned a couple in past years. I did not have much experience with dogs other than Gemi of hunting fame. I knew I did not want another English setter!

I had always admired the German Shepherd dog and felt it a good match for us.

I found a local breeder and she had several pups available. I had heard that female dogs were easiest to train. When I went to the kennel, I told the lady what I thought I wanted and she left. She came back a minute or so later and put this little fluff ball down on the floor!

She ran right up to me and I swear she ran sideways! Her rear end got to me before the head did! I knew then that she was just what I was looking for! I paid for her and she was on her way home!

Laura fell in love with her instantly. We named her Sassy and she became our first four-legged kid! Spoiled rotten but she kept us in laughter for the next decade! Truly a joy.

So far, I was able to perform my job with no problems. Travel still was necessary and I had trade shows to attend as well. I assisted in writing the tech manuals for some of the products and oversaw a refurbishing of returned products.

Typically, I had two or three technicians working on the repairs. There were times that the product returns were coming back in quantities that would overwhelm us. We simply did the best that we could.

There was play too. We lived in a lake community and had access to a lake where fishing and water skiing competed.

We bought a nineteen-foot boat and trailer and did some of both. Friends and family would come up for barbecue's and boating fun nearly every weekend. I never did manage waterskiing but enjoyed hanging out on the boat with a cold beer or driving the others around the lake on tubes or skis. We had some great times. Life was indeed, good.

My good friend Phil and I drove out to the farm in Nebraska so I could pick up my tools and the radial arm saw. We enjoyed the trip and visit to the farm. By now, I had put together a workshop in the basement. It was not very large but I had enough machines and tools to make the things we could use. One of my first projects was a dining room set. I made a two-piece hutch with doors and three drawers. The top part even had stained glass doors.

I had a good source for the wood. I had received a catalog from a wood mill in Pennsylvania. I would pick out what I needed and call it in. The mill would bundle it up and ship it out to me. I had chosen Ash as I liked the weight and feel of it. I continued to build a matching trestle table and four chairs out of the same wood. The chairs eventually had to be replaced but the cabinet and table are still in use twenty-five years later! Over the years, I made a number of furniture pieces out of different woods.

Red Oak was another favorite wood that I used a lot. I designed and built kitchen cabinets and a bedroom piece that has drawers and cabinets, all out of Red Oak.

I built and sold pieces to others as word of mouth got around. I became pretty good at cabinetry as I gained in experience. It was certainly a handy skill to have around an old house!

It was not always easy to perform certain tasks as the disease continued its relentless destruction. Heavy sheets of plywood had to be cut up and I worked alone. I learned to get the sheet of plywood up on the workbench by sliding it up into position. Then, I could use a handheld circular saw and cut the sheet up into manageable pieces. I would then trim the smaller pieces on the table saw with much less effort and keep the cuts very accurate. The phrase, "Necessity is the Mother of Invention" (author unknown) came to mind here. This phrase has become one of my favorites as I learned to compensate or adapt as my upper arm strength ebbed away.

My days were full. I worked, traveled and continued improving around the house. I even managed to go hunting and fishing occasionally. My days working for Bionaire were numbered.

The sales force had oversold the products and because of delayed billing practices, the company was in financial trouble. Product returns soon overwhelmed us. Whole truckloads of used and new product were shipped back to us. With no room to store it, it had to be moved into other temporary warehousing. Layoffs were eminent. It was the first time I had ever been forced to leave a job.

There was a certain level of despair as a result of this layoff. I began to question my own job performance to find a place to put the blame. It was not a good feeling and I knew, deep down, that it was not my fault.

I spent the time working on getting my resume' up to date and sending it out potential employers. I had some interviews but nothing sparked real interest on my part. I spotted a position in the classifieds that got my immediate attention.

Materials Research Corporation was looking for instructors in their training department! This was my old company that I had worked for before I went to college! Excitedly, I sent them my resume'.

A few days later I was called in for a first interview. The company had really grown since my last time there. They had a new large facility at another location. The training department manager interviewed me and it seemed to go well.

Sure enough, soon after, I was called in for a second interview with human resources and others. That too, went smoothly. I was given more detail about the position.

I would be a training instructor on the products they sold. These products were not fifty-dollar air cleaners; they were computer-controlled machines costing in excess of a million dollars each! I was given a salary range and asked if I would be interested. No hesitation on that answer. I felt good about the experience and remember little of the trip home as I thought about the future.

Shortly, I received a call from MRC stating my salary and position offer. I was to report to work the following Monday if I accepted. I had a few days until I started but it was a relief to be gainfully employed once more.

In order to instruct on these complex systems, I had to first learn about them myself. This was no easy task as the machines were highly complex systems that employed ultra-high vacuum, computer and electronic systems. These machines were used in super-clean rooms and had to be kept spotless.

They were used to deposit specialized coatings on silicon substrates that were in turn, used to manufacture integrated circuit chips. We sold these systems to major integrated circuit chipmakers all over the world. A sale of one of these machines generated a need for a training class to teach their technicians how to maintain and repair them. Most of the time, the men from these companies were sent out to us for training. Other times, we would send an instructor out to the manufacturing site and train there.

Once I learned the many systems and understood them, I was assigned classes. Most classes had less than a dozen students and the training was usually a full week long. It was a good experience and I did well.

I was sent to a number of on-site training sessions all over the country. I had to pack up tools, training materials and whatever else was needed and cart it all to the site.

Very often, I had to do the teaching in ultra-clean environments because the machine was already installed in the clean-room settings, undergoing testing and set-up. This involved putting on clean-room clothing that pretty much covered your entire body. Booties and gloves were necessary. Facemasks and hairnets were used. It was often hot and awkward even with the air conditioning. Not very convenient but it was required.

I spent time in Texas, Idaho, California and other places I no longer recall. Once, I was sent to Catania, Italy. This Sicilian city had a full fabrication plant near the outskirts. The experience was memorable for many reasons.

We had our own tech rep on site that supported the new machine but did no training. That was my job. The tech picked me up at the airport upon my arrival and took me to the hotel. Later on, he picked me up and took me to dinner.

I spoke no Italian and English was not spoken by most of the natives so communications were going to be a real challenge. My host spoke passable Italian so I was okay at least for the evening! He was scheduled to go on vacation when I started the training classes. I would be there in Catania for the better part of two weeks and would have two separate classes. In each class, at least one of the students spoke English and translated to the others. It was slow but worked out okay. Once my host departed on his vacation, I was forced to rent a car to get around.

First of all, they drove on the wrong side of the road! Secondly, they only drove flat out. Most were driving the same kind of cars that I had...a tin can Fiat. These things were a very basic vehicle designed as cheap transportation. They were driven with the horn blaring and the accelerator pressed to the floor! Traffic lights were mostly ignored and the lanes, regardless of the direction, were selected based on pure whim! Why there were as few accidents as there were was beyond me. It was worse than I remembered back in Japan.

My first weekend in Catania allowed me to take a drive along the island coast. I went through villages that were very old and very quaint. I was able to drive to the visitors center for the local volcano, Mount St. Etna. This particular volcano was still active and I soon found out just how active!

At night, from my hotel, I could see the red glow and spiral of smoke from the mountain. It was only about ten or so miles away. It seemed to wink at me. No one else seemed concerned so I did not give it a lot of thought either. One night, I was sound asleep in my room when I was awakened. My bed had moved across the room several feet! I thought immediately that Mount Etna had erupted.

As it turned out, it was not the volcano but rather a strong earthquake that had occurred several miles south. Considerable damage and a number of lives were taken on that day. Fortunately, not in my immediate area.

I tried to call both home and office to let them know the details but was not able to get through. It was a day or two later before I finally talked to my boss. He in turn, called and reassured my wife. I was finally able to finish up my training classes and it was time to leave Italy. That big Pan Am Boeing looked real good when I finally was able to board.

Not long later, my boss and friend took ill and passed away. We had a great relationship and I missed him. It was becoming more difficult for me to travel with the tools, manuals, and training aids. The training department was changing with the new manager. I felt a change would be good.

An opening came up for a supervisor's spot in Tech Support. This is where the field reps got support as well as our clients. I would supervise two others but really only worked the phones the same way they did. It went well enough but soon became boring. I did not travel anymore and everyday was like the day before. It eliminated the travel hassles but was not a good scenario for me.

I have never been one to sit back and let the world go by. I needed involvement. When I was teaching, it was dynamic. I had to prepare lessons, relearn systems and find new and better ways to present materials To end up answering the phone and doing minimum research was a let-down. I was ripe for new challenges.

I continued to build furniture for myself and others. I spent many a happy hour in my basement workshop making lots of sawdust.

My health continued to go downhill but at a slow pace. I still could do most of the tasks I set for myself. I did not always do it the conventional way but rather, found other means to get the results I wanted.

I received a phone call from a good friend that I knew from the old Bionaire days. At that time he was the shipping manager when I was the service manager. We had become friends and our wives knew each other. I was surprised as his call was unexpected.

He invited me to lunch and mentioned that he had something that he wanted to discuss with me. I agreed and we soon met for lunch. Pete was now a vice president in the company! Pete then proposed that I come back to work for Bionaire in much the same capacity that I did before. It was more money and Pete would be my immediate boss. A lot had happened and the company was supposedly turned around and profitable again. I would be given free rein to set up the service part as I saw fit. The future was going to be bright and the rewards forthcoming. Like a fool, I bought into it and agreed. I left MRC after a two-week notice and started with Bionaire.

It was around the year 1990 when I was able to fulfil a lifelong dream. I had been going down to the local airport from time to time and got to know a few of the guys.

One of them was a flight instructor and he offered me a demonstration flight for twenty-five dollars. I had flown in small aircraft numerous times before in years gone by. Still, it had been awhile and I decided to take the offer. It was different this time,

We walked out to the Cessna 152 and we did the pre-flight inspection. I was told what to look for and why. We checked fuel, tires and all the flight surfaces before we got into the cockpit. I was directed to sit in the left pilots' seat! This was a first!

I was really excited. Afraid of doing something stupid and causing disaster, I suggested he should probably do this. He just grinned and he showed me what switches to set and where to set the throttle for engine start. With foot on the brakes, I started the engine and the music started!

With his help, I was directed to steer towards the end of the runway where we (he) performed a run-up of the engine and checked the flight controls. All was normal and we taxied onto the end of the runway. I was told to take the controls and accelerated down the runway. Of course, he was following me on the controls and told me when to do what. Soon we were airborne and I was totally hooked. This was just unbelievable!

I began taking lessons. My job was no longer as reprehensible as I looked forward to my next flying lesson. Here I was, nearly fifty years old learning to fly an airplane. What could be better?

Of course, the experience was not without the problems of a man well past his prime! Landings were a definite issue. For some reason, I would botch the last moments before touchdown. When I finally figured out the problem, I would go on and enjoy landings a lot.

Another obstacle that reared its ugly head was performing stalls. This is where you set the aircraft up to the point where it stops flying! It scared the hell out of me. Finally, my instructor got fed up and took me out to the practice area and I stalled the plane over and over again. Finally, I lost my fear and all was well.

This also improved my landings as well. I soloed April, 1991. Wow! I could fly by myself. No one sitting next to me to bail me out! This was a very heady experience! My passion for flying would only grow from that Moment on.

Whenever I got into the plane, taxied to the runway, and launched into the air, life became so much simpler. I did not think about work or children or fixing up the house. I just enjoyed the thrill of flying near the clouds and seeing the tiny figures on the ground. I could see forever and often saw things never seen by those on the ground. It made me feel free and carefree.

Of course, once back on the ground reality would be waiting. But, for a short time, life was without hardship.

The group of guys that were learning to fly at the same time proposed that we buy our own plane. It would be cheaper than renting and the costs would be shared by five of us. Sounded like a good idea and we went ahead.

We located a well-used Cherokee PA-140 made by Piper Aircraft. It was located in Virginia. Jon Berry and I went to check it over and we ended up buying it. N56083 would provide the platform for a bunch of us to get our private pilot's license. I soloed and got my private license while flying this old Piper. I earned my private pilot's license in September 1991.

I now had permission to carry passengers and fly anywhere I wanted. In reality, it was a license to learn how to really fly. I would make mistakes and learn from them. I would practice and practice. Judy, Laura's sister, was my first passenger. I think I was almost as excited as she was. Laura never wanted to fly and she never flew with me. It just was not something she was comfortable with.

My early flights were to familiar areas that I knew well. It would be a bit before I became more adventurous. One new flight experience was to become one of my favorite short trips. This was showed to me by an experienced pilot.

We took off and headed mostly south. Soon, we came to the Hudson River and banked right.

Altitude was adjusted to just under one thousand feet and we proceeded down the river. It was late afternoon and lights were becoming visible. We passed over the George Washington Bridge at eight hundred feet and flew on south pass the skyscrapers of Manhattan and the Palisades along the New Jersey side. We had to look up to see the top of the World Trade Center and Empire State building as we flew along! The statue of Liberty was just to our right.

There was the need to be on the radio and frequently announce our position so that other pilots in the area would know where we were. There was a special frequency reserved for the "river run" to avoid the helicopters and other pilot sightseers.

Flying in the New York/New Jersey area was not easy. Much of it was what was called controlled airspace and you needed special permission to use the area at certain altitudes. Where we were we had to maintain less than one thousand feet but no lower than five hundred. Best you did not lose your focus! However, it was a flight that will always be remembered by anyone who experienced it.

I flew on my birthday, February 7, 1992. I was fifty years old and had achieved a lifelong dream. I was a certified pilot! It is not often that one can achieve things like this and I will always be grateful that I was given the chance. This decade closed on a good note. Life was certainly good!

CHAPTER FIVE

Once bitten by the flying bug, there was a constant urge to fly. We went at the drop of a hat. Any excuse was acceptable. My plane partners and I discussed upgrading the Cherokee to something more complex. We wanted more speed and more capacity. The PA 140 that we had trained on was limited to one passenger unless the third passenger was a child or midget. There was room to sit but the performance limitations of the Cherokee were too restrictive to safely carry a third adult.

One of our friends had located a real nice Beech Craft Debonair that was for sale. If we sold the Cherokee and pooled our money, we could get this plane. It cost more than my house did but what the heck, you only pass by this spot once in a lifetime! It was a beautiful aircraft. It would accommodate four people and was quite a bit faster. We had to each get checked out by a flight instructor in this new aircraft. Endorsement with the Federal

Aviation Agency was required because it had many more features that had to be mastered.

It had retractable landing gear and variable speed propeller that was all new to us. It took off faster, flew faster and landed faster than what we were accustomed to so instruction was essential.

A few hours with our CFI (certified flight instructor) and we got our endorsement. N5861S was a dream ship to fly. It was light on the controls, stable in the air and a real pleasure to fly. It even had an autopilot. The avionics were also more sophisticated. It was capable of navigating on instruments only. Navigation with the loran was a breeze.

I really enjoyed the challenge of finding my way to any new location. Pre-flight planning was the key to this. It was very rewarding to take off, navigate to a locale and hit it accurately. I seldom missed. We flew this aircraft all over the eastern seaboard. The longest trip was to Daytona, Florida. Three of us took turns at the controls getting there. It was great fun.

My dear patient wife lived through this passion of mine with far greater tolerance than I had any right to expect. It was testament to her love and devotion. I could not ask for more from a mate.

I knew I was on borrowed time. My upper arm strength was diminishing and I had problems with proper technique in landing.

The accepted practice is to enter the final leg just before touchdown with your left hand on the control wheel and the right hand on the throttle. As you settled near the runway and flared for the landing, you would pull back on the controls with the left hand and close the throttle all the way with the other. My problem was that my strength had deteriorated to the point that I had to struggle when pulling into the flare. Not a good thing.

I adapted. As I entered the flare and as soon as the throttle was fully closed to idle, I used both hand to finish the flare and my landings were fine. I was smooth and the possible need for immediate landing abort was a simple reverse of the process. I practiced both landing and aborted landing and was satisfied that I could do it safely.

The Debonair was a truly great aircraft. However, it was expensive and some of us were struggling to get the necessary funds to support her. Annual inspections were over two thousand dollars alone. She burned twelve to thirteen gallons per hour only if you leaned her out properly. The old Cherokee only burned six to eight gallons. At over two dollars a gallon, it was a costly thing to fly. None of us were wealthy and the money soon became a serious issue.

It was decided that we would sell her and basically break up our little group. Around October of 1994, the new owner flew her away. That was indeed hard.

One of the guys of our little group, and I gave some thought to finding something that the two of us could afford and was inexpensive to operate. We came across the Grumman AA5.

The Tiger was a fine little airplane. It was almost as fast as the Debonair and was both responsive and light on the controls. It had no steerable nose wheel... you got used to steering with the main brakes easy enough.

There was a local bird that we were able to rent and the cost was reasonable. We got type certified and spent several happy hours flying the little plane.

We tried to find one that we could afford to buy but it just did not happen. I flew the plane less than ten hours total but it was soon sold and we were grounded again. It had been a joy for the short time it lasted.

I flew the flight school Cessna 172 from time to time but renting was just too expensive and I eventually just stopped flying. It was probably time to anyway. I never had a mechanical failure or any accidents in those five years. I attribute that to my excellent training and my own insistence on procedure. I always did my pre-flight inspections and planned my destinations carefully, even if only a short distance away. The only times when things got perilous were times when the weather would change abruptly. I had practiced flying instrument-only flights with a safety pilot and loss of visibility did not terrorize me. I knew what to do if I had to,

By now I was losing the necessary strength to fly safely . It was time to call it a day. The five years that I was allowed to fly will always be with me. No one can take that away from me. It was a short career with only a little less than three hundred hours of total time flying but it was just marvellous. A dream fulfilled. Life was absolutely good!

It was around this time when we brought home four-legged kid number two. Shelby was a real handful as a pup. Black and tan and full of the devil, it took some time to bring her into the fold!

It was in 1995 that I was laid off from Bionaire a second and final time.

Once again, they had fallen into the trap of overselling without upfront payment. Soon we were buried in returned product and inundated with defective claims. It was déjà vu!

My health continued its relentless path of destruction. My right foot, and to a lesser extent, the left foot lost muscle control. I had what was termed "drop foot." I could not lift my foot up at the ankle and consequently, tripped easily if I caught my toe on anything raised. Walking distances were becoming problematic. Long concourse hikes at airports were getting to be a real challenge. I had to learn to anticipate my walking. I mean, I had to place my feet where I wanted them. Something that most people never gave a thought to. Even then, I would catch my toe on some small obstacle and trip.

Finally, I had reached an age where getting rehired was not going to be easy. This was true in most job disciplines. I gave it a good shot and applied for a number of positions. I had several interviews that always went well but never got offers. It became disheartening. I knew that part, if not all of the problem, was my physical condition. It was readily apparent that I had some health issues by the way I moved and walked. It was not real obvious but there nonetheless.

Against all my convictions, it soon became necessary to consider disability retirement. I had worked most of my life and given fair return for fair compensation. I would have strongly preferred that I continue to work. It was just not going to happen. I applied to Social Security for a disability retirement.

This can be a nightmare of an ordeal. I did not experience this. I went through all their forms and filled them out; met with their doctors and subjected myself to their exams and waited. I became eligible to receive monthly payments of disability. That, combined with my small pension from the state from the years I taught school made my income sufficient that I could live with a semblance of dignity. With Laura still working, we were doing pretty well. Certainly, we were better off than many others with similar fates.

Adjustment to an early retirement was not as easy as one would expect. With Laura at work, I had the house to myself and too much quiet. I was used to being with people. I was used to being somewhere. The dynamics of the day were missing. I was fifty-six years old and felt younger. Oh well, move on.

One major advantage that I had was my woodworking. I could lose myself in the shop for hours at a time. I was also an avid reader. I loved to read works of fiction.

I would drop the boat in the lake, take a good book and a few beers and spend a great afternoon floating around the lake while reading. This I could get used to.

One of my good friends from my teaching days, retired from the same school where I had worked. He lived not too far from our house. Phil and his wife Kay, were close friends to both Laura and I. His daughter, Jennifer, is like a daughter to me. Anyway, when he retired, we decided to take a trip out to Arizona and visit my son, Scott. Scott had moved out to Tucson, Arizona a few years earlier and I wanted to see him.

We took the southerly route just for the heck of it and ended up in Nashville. From there we proceeded across Tennessee, Alabama, Mississippi and Louisiana. Once in New Orleans, we then drove across Texas.

This is not so much a state but more like a small country! Hours and hours later, we found ourselves in New Mexico. I love driving across country. The carryover wanderlust was right there.

Phil loved trains and was very knowledgeable about them. We came across trains that were hundreds of cars long and I received intimate knowledge about them all! We would put in a tape and sing to different country and western tunes. We were loud and enthusiastic if not in perfect pitch! It was a fun trip and I cherished the time.

Once in Tucson, we found Scott's apartment. Scott was the consummate host and we ate well and enjoyed the outside Jacuzzi bath. Scott took us around to several area attractions. The desert animal refuge was most notable. They had arranged local flora and fauna in their natural settings in such a way that the public could stroll through the paths and observe them in nearly real settings. It was most impressive.

Time caught up with us and we were soon on our way home. We got an early start and after scraping the frost off of the windshield, we were on our way.

This time we ventured further north to Kansas and made our way across Interstate 70. Soon after, Oberlin, Kansas appeared. It was even more strange to me. It was almost as if I had never been there. A quick look and we were on our way. Our return home was uneventful but we both enjoyed the trip.

I had been going to Englewood Hospital annually for evaluation of my FSHD. The Muscular Dystrophy Association maintained a clinic there. Doctor Meyer was the physician. The only purpose for these visits was to develop a pattern of deterioration. There was not any real way to improve the condition. They evaluated me and I left until next year. I could only hope the data was useful to the researchers of the time. The good doctor has since retired and I no longer participated in these studies.

In 1997, I finally managed to quit smoking. I started this foul habit back when I was in the Air Force. I did not really smoke much then but as the years passed by, I eventually became addicted. By this time, I was a pack a day smoker and the need for a cigarette was always there. I had tried to quit several times before but always came back to them. This time, I did it. Laura still smoked but she also soon gave them up. When I was growing up, smoking was quite acceptable. Lots of folks smoked. Cigarettes were cheap and no stigma was attached to their use. Little did we know just harmful these things really were?

It was around this time when we lost our beloved Sassy. She was thirteen years old and could not get around anymore. I had to stay out in the car in the parking lot at the vet's office when we let her go. I lost it. I cried like a baby. It was one of the most painful things I had ever experienced. It was like losing a child.

Shelby filled the void somewhat but soon, Laura found a little black pup to bring home. She was born on St. Valentine's Day, 1998. This shepherd had to be flown down from someplace in New England. Phil and I drove out to LaGuardia airport to meet and pick her up. This poor thing was scared to death and miserable. It was raining when she flew in and rained for twelve days after. We named her Stormy. She was to become Laura's constant companion.

Our pets filled a void that was ever so important. Laura had made the choice not to have children and with my health issues, this was the right thing to do. The dogs and cats became nearly as important as children. We loved each pet dearly.

Daily life was by now, pretty much routine and uneventful. Laura went to her job and I went to my little shop. I had started to do some of the cooking by now. I was no chef and the meals were pretty simple and straightforward. Much of what I cooked was what I remembered having when growing up. Meat, potatoes and a vegetable were the base. I learned to make soups and both of us enjoyed this. It was pretty simple, healthy and tasty. I used one pot, leftover meat and anything else and the results were really good. In warmer weather, the grill was handy. I used a rotisserie to roast chicken or beef. No muss and no fuss.

I had only an occasional interaction with my kids. I would meet for lunch occasionally with Todd or with Craig. Scott was out in Arizona so I only saw him at Christmas time. Deanna was busy setting up her own career. That was just the way it was. They were busy with their lives and I was never able to become too involved.

It soon became the year 2000. I was now fifty-eight years old. FSHD was an old, if unwanted acquaintance by now. I had to walk carefully, plan out my moves in advance and use alternate ways to accomplish my tasks. I persevered.

Laura and I decided it was time to build a garage attached to the house. We planned an addition that would provide space for the cars and a large room overhead. This would make the house more valuable and we would benefit with more comfort. We had saved most of the money we would need. Permits in hand, we went ahead.

It was a good idea. The cars were protected and we had more room. It was built with two by six lumber and fully insulated so heating it was a cinch.

Shelby the dog was gone by now. Stormy was a few years old and we decided that she needed a sister. The same breeder that sent us Stormy offered us another pup.

It was around this time that I endured another birthday. I became sixty years old in 2002 and another decade bit the dust.

CHAPTER SIX

Supposedly, Samantha was from European stock and had a slightly different look and demeanor. Frankly, I never noticed anything different with her from any of the other shepherds I had known. Like all beings, no two were alike and this new pup was no exception. I had driven up to Maine to pick her up when she was about six weeks old in March of 2002. We named her Samantha but she was always Sam or Sammy. She was a typical black and tan shepherd and came with the full complement of adorable. I do not think Stormy was all that impressed with her but everyone else took to her instantly.

I made every effort to keep up a positive outlook on everything. I still kept active and worked making such things as small cabinets and other endeavors. My projects were smaller and less physically demanding but still satisfying. I even managed to install the oak banister and railing in the new addition. I produced the trim moldings and installed them.

I walked without aid though more carefully. I tired more easily and had to sit down more often. My sense of balance was impaired and an occasional fall was not unusual. By now, my right leg was showing signs of weakening. I rarely got hurt in these tumbles as I fell without being rigid. It was a small advantage due to the loss of muscle.

More importantly, I was still able to regain my feet without assistance from another person. The worst problem was how it affected my confidence. I was slowly turning ultra-cautious. Over all though, my general health was still good. Things could be worse.

I had little contact with my children. An occasional lunch and the annual Christmas eve dinner were about the extent of it. I suppose I would have to accept the blame for this as I was not aggressive in getting involved in their lives. I have always harbored guilt for not being there for the grandkids. It reminded me too much of my own relationship with my father. Before I would know it, I would not be able to do much participation even if I wanted to. As I mentioned before, I was not always proud of myself. My only solace was in the knowledge that I was very proud of them all and loved them without any reserve. I bragged about them every chance I got.

This decade would see the passing of some very close lives. The first shock was the sudden death of my friend, Phil's wife Kay. She was around my age and for all we knew in good health. The next we knew she was gone from an apparent heart attack. She and Laura had become very close over the years. It was a sad time. Her daughter, Jennifer was devastated. Phil handled it all with stoic calm. Next year would bring on the next tragic event.

My mother in law, Laura's Mom, and I had become close over the years. She loved to come up on weekends to work in our yard. She and Laura would work outside for hours at a time planting flowers and making the place look nice. When she took ill with diabetes and needed more help, it was decided that she would come stay with us. 1

We had a small bedroom built for her and tried to make her feel at home. She resisted the dialysis and needed firm direction from Laura to make sure she received the necessary treatments. It was not long before this became a difficult problem.

My wife was working full time and needed to insure that her mother was getting the necessary care. Mom was growing weaker and more contrite. I was not able to do much for her in my situation. If she fell, I would be unable to do much to help her.

Laura discussed it with her siblings and it was decided that a nursing home was the only practical solution. It was a very difficult decision but one that had to be made. It was in July 2005 that Dawn Pfitzner passed away. She was a grand lady and would be missed.

There was little to reflect on in the ensuing years. No more real life's events occurred until 2008. I was experiencing an abnormal amount of coughing and hoarseness. It was time for me to seek some medical help.

I scheduled a visit with a specialist in the throat area. Doctor Remsen examined me and took my health history. He performed an endoscope procedure where he inserted a small tube into my throat area and recorded pictures of my throat. He found signs of a dark growth on my larynx. A small biopsy of the tissue would soon prove that the area was cancerous and would have to be removed. My years of smoking had, at long last, caught up with me, even after having given them up so many years ago.

I was soon scheduled into the hospital and the growth was surgically removed. I then had to undergo six weeks of radiation therapy where they radiated the throat area five days per week. Being scared was the least of it. I had burns around my throat and side effects started to manifest themselves.

This was not something I needed. FSHD should have been more than my share of coping! Foods that were always tasty before were becoming less so. My mouth became excessively dry. My voice changed subtly and I could not talk very long without going hoarse and nearly losing my voice.

These were to be permanent changes. Even so, after stipulated examinations every six months for the next five years, I thankfully, remained cancer free. Another of life's obstacles had been overcome. Life was still pretty good.

In 2010, we lost the Storm dog. She was twelve years old and Laura's best sidekick. She finally took ill and could not get around anymore. With much regret, we decided to help her maintain her dignity and let her go. Never easy. Stormy would be missed as well.

The next couple of years were simply routine. The FSHD was continuing its relentless path of destruction. My legs were now getting pretty weak. Abdominal strength was noticeably worse as well. My sense of balance had become very unstable. If I got out of balance, I simply fell. Getting back on my feet was very difficult as well. My best solution was to make my way over to a staircase and get my feet lower than my body. Stairs were not always available and I would need someone to help me.

It was a scary time. I knew that this horrific condition was going to win. I also knew I would not give up without a fight! I involved myself with organizations devoted to curing this malady. I registered with "National Registry of Myotonic Dystrophy & FSHD Patients and Family Members". It was located at the University of Rochester in New York. This was a database used by doctors and researchers to obtain both data and volunteers for their research.

I also was enrolled in the "Muscular Dystrophy Association." Sometime later, I joined the "FSH Society." It was this organization that offered the most hope and the most direct information as to the findings for FSHD.

I liked that it was devoted to the cure of the Facioscapulohumeral Muscular Dystrophy and offered more promise than any other group.

There was little else left of this decade worth mentioning. My struggles were still there facing me each day. Laura continued with her work and caring for our home. Those things around the house that needed attention we worked at together. She became quite adept at simple repairs with my input. Those things beyond our abilities would be set aside until we could find someone to do them.

Hiring people to get jobs done was like betting on the lottery. The chances of getting the job done and done right had long odds. I wondered what had happened to the old and valued work ethic!

It was time to put this decade to bed. I turned seventy. It was February 7, 2012.

CHAPTER SEVEN

As this story draws nearer to the end I will not write about the future but only convey the final description of my condition and leave on a positive note.

By this time I walked with aids. I could only take short steps without the assistance of a cane or something solid to grab onto. I resisted going to the walker for as long as I could and used a cane to manage. My balance had become so precarious that the cane soon was not enough security. Finally accepting the walker, I felt more secure in walking short distances.

Longer treks I managed quite well using my lightweight scooter that was battery powered. Before this newer scooter, I had an earlier model scooter that was much too heavy for either me or my wife to get into the car. I used this around the house and it was great.

The new one, however, was an aluminum framed unit powered by a lithium ion battery. It collapsed into a small size and only weighed about thirty-five pounds. Laura could lift it easily into the car and even I could still manage to get it in and out of the car myself. Admittedly, it was a bit of a struggle for me. Still, it was a vital aid.

Medicare assisted me in obtaining a powered wheel chair not too long ago. I do not rely on it much yet but will in the not too distant future. We had an access ramp built into the front door of the house. These are truly great devices and help you keep your independence.

I assume that if you are reading this you either have the diagnosis or are close to someone who does. At any rate, the following comments are my observations.

It is sometimes hard to accept the need for assistance whether it is from people or the use of mechanical aids. Get over it and move on. Do what has to be done and do not worry about anything else. I have found most people are very caring and will go out of their way to assist you. Be gracious and accept it. They get more from it than you do!

By now, you have evolved into an on-the-fly inventor. You have become a master of adaptation. Using two hands to brush your teeth is second nature. Glue (waterproof) a piece of sponge on a stick and you can reach difficult places to apply lotion or soap. Have grab bars installed everywhere; in the shower, near doors, wherever you need them.

Finally, keep yourself occupied. Find something you like to do and do it. I have worked with my hands most of my life.

I still do. I have a small shop in my basement with a few tools that I use to make things that I give away. I buy quality knife blades and put on hardwood handles. I make a leather sheath for it and folks love them. I get enough to pay for the materials and all is well.

I also have a small bench top lathe that I can turn small wooden objects on. These are often gifts that I make for friends and family. Most of these activities I can do sitting down. I cannot do it for long periods but rather over time, I get some pretty good results. More importantly, I feel like I am doing something worthwhile. The more you do the more you can do.

There is a deadly trap waiting for you. If you choose to give into the condition and simply sit around watching television, you will grow weaker. The weaker you become, the less you will want to do. Do you see the trap?

On the last page, I will list the various organizations and companies that should be recognized. They offer products, services and up to date information. There is real progress being made in FSHD research. The sooner there is a cure the better.

I will soon become seventy-one years old. Life is still good. I hope it will be for you too. I have no way of knowing what the future holds for me but I hope I can face it head on and continue to go forward.

Remember, there is always someone out there with worse troubles than you have!

Resources

Services and Information Sources

FSH Society, Inc.

BBRI R353

64 Grove Street

Watertown, MA 02472

www.fshsociety.org

(617) 658-7878

The FSH Society should be joined and followed closely for new research and developments. A valuable source of information.

Muscular Dystrophy Association

National Headquarters

3300 E. Sunrise Drive

Tucson, AZ 85718

www.mda.org

(800) 572-1717

The MDA offers information and provides a monthly magazine containing cur-rent news and other articles. This is free. There is usually a local MDA office in larger cities where you can turn to for direct assistance.

National Registry of Myotonic & FSHD

601 Elmwood Avenue, Box 673

Rochester, NY 14642-8673

www.urmc.rochester.edu

(888) 925-4302

The National Registry is part of the University of Rochester Medical Center and provides access to information on patients for researchers. to contact. In some situations the patient will be asked to participate in their research efforts. You will be given a lengthy form to fill out and be put in the database if you volunteer. It can only help.

Mobility Resources

Hoveround Corporation

6010 Cattleridge Drive

Sarasota, FL 34232

www.hoveround.com

(800) 771-6565

They offer mobility scooters and chairs that are reasonably priced. They work closely with you in obtaining funding from Medicare or other insurances. I have the power chair.

TravelScoot USA

504 Kirkland Road

Chehalis, WA 98532

www.travelscoot.com

(800) 342-2214

This company offers an ultra-light scooter made of aluminum. It folds into a compact size and only weights about thirty-five pounds with the optional lithium ion battery. I keep it in my car for when I go shopping and other activities. It is airport/plane friendly.

Acorn Stair lifts

7335 Lake Ellenor Drive

Orlando, FL 32809

www.acornstairlifts.com

(888) 212-8995

If your home is on more than one level, this is an ideal solution.

Discount Ramps

760 S. Indiana Avenue

West Bend, WI 53095

www.discountramps.com

(888)651-3431

The company offers every style ramp and lift imaginable. They can be ordered on-line. Access to your home and car is much easier with one of these.

Made in the USA
Charleston, SC
21 June 2013